D1571330

The
Heritage
of American Catholicism

A TWENTY-EIGHT-VOLUME SERIES DOCUMENTING THE HISTORY
OF AMERICA'S LARGEST RELIGIOUS DENOMINATION

EDITED BY

Timothy Walch

ASSOCIATE EDITOR
U.S. Catholic Historian

A Garland Series

The Diverse Origins of American Catholic Education

CHICAGO, MILWAUKEE, AND THE NATION

TIMOTHY WALCH

Garland Publishing, Inc.
New York & London
1988

LIBRARY OF CONGRESS CATALOGING-IN-PUBLICATION DATA

Walch, Timothy, 1947-
The diverse origins of American Catholic education

(The Heritage of American Catholicism)
Bibliography: p.
1. Catholic schools—United States—History.
2. Catholic Church—Education—United States—History.
I. Title. II. Series.
LC501.W27   1988   377'.82'73   88-24360
ISBN 0-8240-4102-X (alk. paper)

DESIGN BY MARY BETH BRENNAN

PRINTED ON ACID-FREE, 250-YEAR-LIFE PAPER.
MANUFACTURED IN THE UNITED STATES OF AMERICA

In Memory of My Parents

Margaret M. DeSchryver
and
George L. Walch

CONTENTS

PREFACE

Questions about Catholic schools are prominent in the lively debate over private education. Do Catholic schools provide better cognitive outcomes and better personality and character development than public schools? Do Catholic schools provide a safer, more disciplined, more ordered environment than public schools? Are Catholic schools socially divisive? Is it constitutional for parents of Catholic school students to receive tax credits for tuition payments? These and other questions concern government officials and the media as well as draw the attention of sociologists and other social scientists.

Surprisingly, the subject has not appealed very much to historians. That there have been only four historical surveys of Catholic parochial schools written since 1900 qualifies the topic as one of the most neglected in American historiography. Early in this century, James A. Burns published the first work on Catholic schools and the fact that his two volumes are still in use is a testament to the lack of scholarship in the field. Bernard Kohlbrenner abridged Burns' work in 1937 and transformed the two volumes into "a textbook for normal schools and teachers colleges." He also added several chapters of his own to bring the story up to date. A third general history appeared in 1970. Its author, Harold A. Buetow, provided extensive annotation, but relied almost exclusively on previously published sources. Glen

Gabert published the most recent study in 1973 and claimed that his brief history was an analysis of the official policies that have directed the schools to the present day. None of these four histories offered the depth of research or the sophisticated analysis that the topic demands.

This book seeks to expand the historical understanding of the diverse origins of the Catholic parochial schools in America. It focuses on the formative years of Catholic education in the nineteenth century, comparing the experiences of eastern dioceses such as Boston and New York with two midwestern dioceses, Chicago and Milwaukee.

These latter two cities were chosen for study because they were communities of similar origin and provided a contrast to eastern cities. Their growth from settlements to cities in the nineteenth century resulted from the agricultural and industrial expansion of the Old Northwest in the decades after 1840. Their strategic locations on the western shore of Lake Michigan made them important links in the transportation system of westward expansion. Both communities adopted charters in the late 1830s, added a variety of urban services in the 1840s, and became major cities by the mid-1850s.

These cities also became major centers of the American Catholic population. Chicago and Milwaukee became dioceses in the same year, 1843, and archdioceses within five years of one another. The bishops of these communities shared many of the same problems, opportunities, and accomplishments. Most importantly, both communities experienced a rapid and sustained growth in their parochial school populations. By the turn of the century, the two midwestern archdioceses were educating almost 10 percent of all the children enrolled in Catholic parochial schools in the United States.

Yet the development of these Catholic communities was not identical and their individual stories also demand careful consideration. Chicago was an ethnically diverse diocese administered by a string of bishops who were unable to exercise much control over their parishes. The Germans and the French, for example, were virtually independent of the bishops of Chicago during the middle years of the century. Patrick A. Feehan, named first Archbishop of Chicago in 1880, finally began to centralize the administration of the sprawling archdiocese during the last two decades of the nineteenth century, but the task was not completed until the tenure of George Mundelein in the 1920s. The first fifty years of Catholicism in Chicago were tumultuous, seldom resembling the stereotype of an efficient, bureaucratic denomination.

Catholicism and Catholic education in Milwaukee was far different from that in Chicago due in large part to one man, John Martin Henni. A Swiss-born German, Henni ruled over Milwaukee from the establishment of the diocese in 1843 until his death in 1879. Henni was fortunate to lead a diocese that was overwhelmingly German; he did not face the inter-ethnic hostility that so plagued the bishops of Chicago. Henni organized parishes, established a seminary, opened a teachers college, supported a hospital and several asylums, and financed the North American head-

quarters of an order of German nuns. Good health and good for-
tune allowed him to lead his diocese without major conflict for
more than thirty-five years.

The chapters that follow describe the evolutionary patterns
of Catholic parochial education in the United States and the distinct aspects of parish school development in Chicago and Milwaukee. Above all, the book points to the fact that Catholic education in the nineteenth century was not a seamless garment, but a
patchwork of different diocesan experiences. It was not until
the 1920s that the Church in the United States could generalize
about the patterns of parochial school development.

ACKNOWLEDGEMENTS

This book began as a dissertation at Northwestern University and has benefited from the ideas and comments of many historians, librarians, and archivists. I am especially grateful for the assistance of the dozens of individuals in libraries and archives across the country who assisted me in my research. In particular, I would like to acknowledge the continuing assistance of Archie Motley, curator of manuscripts at the Chicago Historical Society and dean of Chicago historical resources.

Many historians were generous in commenting on all of the chapters of the manuscript at various stages of its preparation. Robert L. Church and Henry Binford, both of Northwestern University, and George M. Frederickson of Stanford University, commented on the first draft. Michael W. Sedlak of Michigan State University, James W. Sanders of the College of Staten Island, City University of New York, and Edward R. Kantowicz, formerly of Carleton University in Canada, commented on a subsequent version. The assistance of all of these men substantially improved the quality of the chapters that follow.

Other scholars shared their ideas on selected chapters. Chapter I benefited from the careful review of John Tracy Ellis and Robert Trisco, both of the Catholic University of America, and Vincent P. Lannie, formerly of the University of Notre Dame. Chapter IV was reviewed by Christopher J. Kauffman, editor of the

U. S. Catholic Historian, Dolores A. Liptak of Catholic Archival and Historical Services, and M. Felicitas Powers, formerly of the Archives of the Archdiocese of Baltimore. Chapter VII is better for the careful review and evaluation of Randolph C. Miller and the editorial board of Religious Education. For the support and guidance of these scholars, the author is most grateful.

Earlier versions of several chapters appeared as essays in scholarly journals. For their permission to reprint this material, the author wishes to acknowledge the American Catholic Historical Association, the U. S. Catholic Historical Society, the Religious Education Association, and the Chicago Historical Society.

Finally, the publication of this book would not have been possible without the support and encouragement of my wife, Victoria Irons Walch. Along with our children, she makes it all worthwhile.

INTRODUCTION

THE VARIETY OF AMERICAN CATHOLIC EDUCATIONAL EXPERIENCES

I

The story of American Catholic education is not easy to summarize because there were many different responses to the questions of how to educate Catholic children. These responses were determined by the economic and social development of Catholic communities within different dioceses, by the quality and effectiveness of the various leaders of those dioceses, and by the attitudes of Catholic parents toward education.

Certainly the bishops strongly supported parochial education. Beginning at the first provincial council of Baltimore in 1829, and at seven succeeding provincial and plenary councils, the bishops admonished, pleaded, and finally demanded that Catholics establish and support parish schools.[1] But the effectiveness of these bishops as leaders of individual dioceses and the laity's response to their calls for schools were far from uniform.

---

1. Neil G. McCluskey, ed., Catholic Education in America: A Documentary History (New York, 1964), pp. 51-64, 78-94. McCluskey provides an excellent selection of documents that reveal the support of Catholic bishops and other leaders for parochial education. Included in the volume are the relevant passages on education from the provincial and plenary councils of Baltimore, 1829 to 1884.

American Catholic education was, in fact, a patchwork of different diocesan experiences. In Boston, for example, most Catholics were indifferent to the establishment of parish schools. A few hundred miles to the southwest, however, New York bishop John Hughes and his flock made parish schools one of their highest priorities. Halfway across the country, Chicago Catholics struggled to build parish schools and still remain active in the public educational establishment of their new rising metropolis. No two dioceses responded in quite the same way to the call for parish schools.

What accounts for these diocesan differences within a denomination that had a reputation for law and discipline? Like many organizations, the Church in the United States was affected by many factors beyond its control. First, the social and economic development of a diocese had a substantial effect on the history of Catholic education in that city. In some dioceses, Catholics were restricted to lower class occupations and lived in slum neighborhoods; in other dioceses, Catholics were scattered among all the social classes and served as urban leaders.

Second, relations between Catholics and non-Catholics affected parochial school development. In some dioceses, controversy over the content of public education led to the establishment of parish schools. In other dioceses, parochial education seemed to supplement an overburdened public school system. In still other dioceses, Catholics saw little need for parish schools and ignored the bishops' plea for such institutions.

Third, the quality of episcopal leadership was an important factor. Some bishops were able to build a school in almost every parish; other bishops failed or did not care. Those who succeeded in this effort knew well that the support and involvement of pastors, sister-teachers, and parishioners were vital to the campaign.

Beyond these generalizations, it is important to remember that the parish was the fundamental component of parochial school development. Here again, the content of the Catholic classroom varied from parish to parish as well as from diocese to diocese. The various manifestations of all these factors fit together to tell the story of American Catholic education in the nineteenth century.

II

Historical scholarship on Catholic education has tended to generalize from the experiences of a single diocese -- New York. Certainly that diocese is one useful case study of parochial school development. But to gain a better perspective on the New York experience one needs to contrast it with the story of parochial school development in other dioceses. It is only through such a comparison that it is possible to appreciate the uniqueness of different diocesan school systems.

Nineteenth century Boston is a good example of how the same set of factors led to a parochial school system very different from the one in New York. When large numbers of Catholics began arriving in Boston in the decades after 1820, they entered a city with an old tradition of anti-Catholicism. It was illegal for Catholics to even practice their faith in that city until 1780; they could not hold public office until 1820; and they were required to pay taxes for the support of Protestantism until 1833.

In the face of this hostility, Boston Catholics -- the bishops as well as the laity -- consciously avoided any actions that would further antagonize the general populace. "The pursuit of peace at almost any price necessarily obviated any strong advocacy of parochial schools," notes historian James Sanders of Bishop John Fitzpatrick. "Instead, his policy of appeasement and hopes for a better day swung the balance in favor of public schools. Perhaps through the public schools his Catholics could gain acceptance as he had done."[2]

But poor relations between Catholics and non-Catholics was not the only factor that undermined parochial education in Boston. The lack of leadership also contributed to the malaise. Boston Catholics -- bishops, priests, and laity -- showed very little interest in parish schools. The bishops gave top priority to the establishment of enormous churches -- monuments to the presence of Catholicism in a Protestant city. The laity, among the poorest immigrants to arrive in this country, accepted this decision and funneled their meager earnings into the construction of monumental church structures. It seems that in Boston, the

2. James W. Sanders, "Boston Catholics and the School Question, 1825-1907," in James W. Fraser, Henry L. Allen, and Sam Barnes, eds., From Common School to Magnet School: Selected Essays in the History of Boston's Schools (Boston, 1979), p. 62. See also Donna Merwick, Boston's Priests, 1848-1910 (Cambridge, 1973) for a discussion of the Catholic clergy in New England and their relations with urban Protestant elites.

construction of a large church was an acceptable form of religious expression, but the establishment of a parochial school was
not. "The financial respectability they could not achieve as individuals could be simulated through their churches," notes
Sanders. "In a Yankee society that associated wealth with virtue, opulent churches seemed necessary. The squat school-
churches, utilitarian but ugly, would never do in Boston."[3]   It
was an extraordinary pastor and a very generous parish that was
willing to build both a church and a school.

The history of Catholic education in New York differed significantly from that in Boston. In fact, New York became known as
"the center of the parochial school movement" in the United
States. Yet the same factors that had affected the educational
experiences of Catholics in Boston also shaped the parochial
schools of New York. The results, however, were quite different.

New York Catholics also found a Protestant city when they
arrived in the 1820s. But unlike Boston's Catholics, New York's
Catholics did not cower at the state of affairs; they fought
against the injustices they remembered from their native lands.
Bishop John Hughes, a man who deeply distrusted the Protestant
majority, exploited the tension and used it to solidify his hold
over his flock. "In some respects," Hughes wrote of the nativists and other anti-Catholics, "their violence was very service-
able to the Catholic cause."[4]

---

3. Sanders, "Boston Catholics and the School Question," p. 58.

4. John Hughes to Prefect, March 23, 1858, Archives of the
University of Notre Dame, as cited in Jay P. Dolan, The Immigrant

The tension was manifest in 1840-42, during a two-year debate that began over the distribution of public funds to parochial schools.[5]   Led by Hughes, New York Catholics petitioned the city council for a share of the city's state school fund allocation. In defense of the claim, Hughes argued that Catholic parents would not in good conscience send their children to the public schools because Catholic students were required to read from the King James Bible and use textbooks that openly criticized Catholicism. He further reasoned that Catholic parents had every right to use their share of the school fund to support their own schools.

But Hughes and his flock were rebuffed by the city council and later by the state assembly; there would be no state funds for parish schools. "How are we to provide for the Catholic education of our children?" he asked. "I answer: Not by agitating the question of the constitutionality, legality, or expediency of State schools. Let us leave these points to be settled by the politicians. Let us leave the public schools to themselves."[6]

Diocesan leadership was also very different in New York than in Boston. "In New York no one had to ask who ruled the Church:

Church: New York's Irish and German Catholics, 1815-1865 (Baltimore, 1975), p. 162.

5. Vincent P. Lannie provides the more complete discussion of the school controversy and its aftermath. See Lannie, Public Money and Parochial Education: Bishop Hughes, Governor Seward and the New York School Controversy (Cleveland, 1968) and Lannie, "Alienation in America: The American Catholic Immigrant in Pre-Civil War America," Review of Politics 32 (September, 1970): 503-521. Also of value is Carl F. Kaestle, The Evolution of an Urban School System: New York City, 1750-1850 (Cambridge, 1973).

6. New York Freeman's Journal, December 15, 1849; Lannie, Public Money and Parochial Education, pp. 245-258.

John Hughes was boss. He believed that the city demanded a 'new mode of government' in the church and that of necessity he had to be both 'bishop and chief.'"[7] In this capacity, Hughes ordered the establishment of parish schools and he was obeyed.

Hughes' force of will was not the only reason for the positive response to parochial education in New York. The New York laity were a mixture of Irish and German immigrants that seemed to be more inclined to support parish schools than their brethren in Boston. They tended to eschew big churches and put their money into schools. Indeed, they saw the schools as a means of transmitting both Catholic culture and national heritage to their young children. In time, the New York parish schools became less ethnic and more American in content, but they remained distinctly Catholic and popular with the laity.

The transition from ethnic to American values in parochial education was also evident in New York's parish schools. In a effort to compete effectively with the public schools, New York Catholics shaped a curriculum that was very similar to that used in the public schools. In fact, many parish schools outdid their public counterparts in their emphasis on patriotism and Americanism. "Catholic apologists were working overtime to demonstrate the compatibility of their religion with the democratic system."[8]

---

7. Dolan, Immigrant Church, p. 164.

8. Ibid., p. 162.

III

Catholic education in the emerging cities of the upper Middle West was yet another educational experience -- one different from that in Boston or New York. When the Catholic Church came to the Middle West in the 1840s, Chicago and Milwaukee reflected both a present and a future. On the one hand they were frontier communities with few of the amenities necessary for comfortable urban life. In fact, they were little more than trading centers on the western shore of Lake Michigan. On the other hand, they were also cities of great optimism, where every citizen took pride in his community. As Stanley Elkins and Eric McKitrick pointed out more than thirty years ago, "this was the setting in which intolerance could not be permitted to interfere with promotion: the organizer must be free to boast of schools and churches for all."[9] Thus the citizens of early Chicago and Milwaukee perceived the establishment of Catholic schools as part of the larger advancement of their communities. Many non-Catholics applauded and supported these efforts.

Such cooperation certainly surprised the bishops of these new dioceses, especially those who had received their training in the East. Bishop William Quarter of Chicago was surprised when he found "that a spirit of great liberality exists toward Catho-

---

9. Stanley Elkins and Eric McKitrick, "A Meaning for Turner's Frontier: Democracy in the Old Northwest," Political Science Quarterly 69 (September, 1954): 348.

lics in all parts of this state."[10]   In contrast with the situation in New York and Boston, the institutional role of the Church in Chicago and Milwaukee was important because it established a tradition of Catholic involvement in urban affairs almost from these cities' inception. As these cities grew, Catholic social institutions became less visible, but the tradition of commitment still remained. The Church was intensely involved in all facets of community life.

The cooperative relationship did not last forever, of course. Once other groups began to establish similar social institutions, the impact of the Catholic contribution declined. In fact, the relationship became downright acrimonious. But when local Catholic leaders objected to public education, non-Catholics listened carefully. Moreover, persistent defeats in the political sector did not deter or discourage these Catholics from their campaign for a share of the school fund. Throughout the nineteenth century, they petitioned and lobbied for what they believed were their rights as citizens. Occasionally, their voice made a difference in the kind and quality of education offered in Chicago and Milwaukee. This dialogue on education was part of a political tradition based on bargain and compromise.

Implicit in this perpetual conflict was a certain degree of mutual respect. Even though Catholics and non-Catholics did not convince one another of the merits of their respective arguments, both sides made certain policy changes to meet each other's

10. William Quarter to John Baptist Purcell, September 2, 1844, Archives of the University of Notre Dame (hereinafter cited as UNDA).

criticism. The catalyst for these changes was the productive tension that existed between the Catholic and non-Catholic communities of Chicago and Milwaukee.

Recent historical scholarship has underscored the fact that frontier communities frequently have exhibited significant amounts of tension over social issues. This was due in large part to the fact that no one group had exclusive political or economic control of the community. Different factions within these communities had to deal with each other as equals and work out their differences in public debate. It was an open and fluid, if acrimonious, process.[11]

Chicago and Milwaukee were frontier communities in the 1840s and 1850s when the Church became involved in urban affairs and commenced the arguments over public education. Both Catholic and non-Catholic leaders emphasized the importance of the schools and not only for the transmission of knowledge. "Catholic parochial schools were not designed to "educate in the literal and classical sense of the term," notes Paul Kleppner, "but to socialize the group into a specific value system . . . . Once we realize that the common school system was established for precisely the same reason, to inculcate a specific set of values, we can appreciate the persistence of the conflicts between

---

11. George M. Frederickson, "Settlers and 'Savages' on Two Frontiers," New York Review of Books (March 18, 1982): 51-54; Howard Lamar and Leonard Thompson, eds., The Frontier in History: North America and South Africa Compared (New Haven, 1981).

Catholics and [non-Catholics] over 'education.'"[12]   The two
groups balanced one another and this process stimulated change.

Church-state relations was not the only factor affecting
parochial school development. Relations between bishops and parishes in Chicago and Milwaukee were also important in determining
the fate of parochial education. One church official disclosed
that "when a pastor undertakes to erect a parochial school he
meets with three classes of persons in his parish; the upper
class which he cannot force, the middle class which he is able to
force, and the poor people who are in favor of it."[13]   Diversity
of opinion, rather than unanimity, was the Catholic response to
the school question in Chicago and Milwaukee.

This diversity also had an ethnic expression that was en-
demic to many American dioceses. Oscar Handlin once noted that
Catholic peasants in Europe had a reverential respect for their
priests and bishops.[14]   But when these groups migrated to the
urban Middle West, they certainly did not expect priests and
bishops of another nationality. The American priesthood and
episcopacy were predominantly Irish by 1860, but the laity was a
mixture of Germans, French, Italians, and Poles as well as the
Irish. When an Irish prelate dictated to a non-Irish parish, the
result was often disobedience. Even more disruptive was any
attempt to assign a priest of one nationality to a parish whose

---

12. Paul Kleppner, The Cross of Culture (Glencoe, Ill., 1971),
pp. 172–173.

13. Quoted in Daniel P. Reilly, The School Controversy
(Washington, 1943), p. 260.

14. Oscar Handlin, The Uprooted (Boston, 1952), pp. 117–139.

members were of another nationality. To keep the peace many diocese became patchworks of ethnic parishes united only by physical proximity. Not surprisingly, educational decisions in Chicago and Milwaukee were often made on the parish level.

The importance of ethnicity as a factor in the origins of Catholic education should not be minimized. For many immigrant parents, the parochial school was not only a means of educating their children and preparing them for the work force. The school was also a mechanism for preserving both religious faith and cultural traditions, two commodities that immigrant Catholics held dear to their hearts. "A man holds dear what little is left," wrote Oscar Handlin, "when much is lost, there is no risking the remainder."[15]

Not every ethnic Catholic group was ardent in its support of parochial schools. The Italians, for example, never showed much interest. Yet the other major ethnic groups, particularly the Germans and the Poles, worked very hard to establish schools in each of the parishes. They worked equally hard to keep their schools independent of any outside influences. "Within these communities," adds Jay P. Dolan, "the school became a key part of the local parish culture and the common place crusade to preserve culture through religion strengthened its importance."[16] Parents, pastors, and sister-teachers worked together to develop the curriculum. The bishop was rarely consulted about such matters.

---

15. Ibid., p. 117.

16. Dolan, Immigrant Church, p. 277.

This is not to say that the bishop had no influence over parish school development. In fact, the operation of Catholic schools in these two dioceses was linked inextricably to the working relationship that existed between the bishops and their parishes. As if to dramatize the variety of possible experiences, the two dioceses reflect contrasting histories.

In Chicago, the working relationship was tumultuous for the first twenty-five years. Predominantly Irish bishops attempted to regulate unilaterally German, French, and Irish parishes and each time these prelates met heavy resistance. It was not until the 1870s, when Bishop Thomas Foley shared his authority with his parishes, that peace came to the diocese. Foley understood the importance of the parish not only as a form of organization but also as a decision-making body.

This was a lesson that the first bishop of Milwaukee, John Henni, learned very quickly. By consulting the pastors and the councils of his German and Irish parishes, the Swiss-born Henni generally avoided the uproar that existed in Chicago. Yet this peace depended entirely on Henni remaining as bishop. The appointment of a German-born successor caused a great clamor among the Irish who feared a move toward "Germanization." Both communities were made archdioceses by 1880 and overcame some of their localism with the establishment of diocesan school boards. Yet the parish remained the center of educational decision-making well into the twentieth century.

A final factor that defined the Catholic educational experience was the curriculum. Some educators in recent years

have argued that the parochial schools were at odds with American
social values in the nineteenth and early twentieth centuries.
"I personally think that the Catholic schools and the Catholic
Church in general," wrote one school superintendent in the pages
of America, "have rendered very significant service to American
society by being at times radically countercultural and I think
it is essential that we continue to be so in the new societal
context of the twentieth century."[17]   Those who argue this position point to religious and foreign language instruction as evidence of their claim and their argument is not without merit.
But such arguments lose some of their force when one examines the
content and the social values of nineteenth-century Catholic
schoolbook.

Even though many Catholics in Chicago and Milwaukee rejected
the concept of a common education for all citizens, they did not
condemn the American values that permeated the public school curriculum.   In fact, an examination of Catholic and public school
textbooks shows a remarkable similarity between the two. Popular
themes -- the educational value of nature, the superiority of the
American way of life, the importance of "proper" social behavior
-- appeared in Catholic as well as public texts. Within this
framework, both types of books emphasized such values as patriotism, religious devotion, parental respect, thrift, honesty, and
diligence.   The one point of deviation between the two was the
past. While public school histories tended to ignore the Catho-

---

17. Michael O'Neill, "Countercultural Schools," America 126
(April 1, 1972): 351-352.

lic contribution to American life, the Catholic texts over-
emphasized the role of the Church.

Certainly an examination of textbooks does not give a complete picture of the nineteenth century classroom. Yet the importance of these books and their message cannot be ignored. As
Sam Bass Warner has noted, "the goal of literacy, both Catholic
and secular, for any child who presented himself at the school
door meant that the Catholic Church was a securely tied to the
task of Americanization as were the contemporary public
schools."[18]

IV

"The story of the first Catholic schools in Milwaukee and
Chicago," wrote James A. Burns, "recalls the early school history
of New York, Baltimore and Boston."[19]   The first historian of
American Catholic education, Burns was in error. Not only were
the parochial educational experiences of Chicago and Milwaukee
different from those in these eastern dioceses, but there were
also differences between Catholic schooling in New York, Baltimore, and Boston. Burns also argued that "there was no question
with the laity as to the wisdom of attempting to establish a
separate system of Catholic schools. Like their pastors, the
laity accepted this alternative as a matter of course."[20]   As in

18. Sam Bass Warner, Jr., The Urban Wilderness (New York,
1972), p. 166.

19. James A. Burns, The Growth and Development of the Catholic
School System in the United States (New York, 1912), p. 15.

20. Ibid., p. 16.

the first instance, Burns was wrong here as well. He glossed over or ignored the very real differences in parochial education from one diocese to another and even from one parish to another.

We might forgive Father Burns for his excessive zeal, however. As an advocate of parochial education in an era of renewed anti-Catholicism, Burns felt compelled to defend his Church and emphasize its unity of purpose. Published in 1908 and 1912, his two volumes on the development of parochial education were more apologetics than history. Unfortunately successive generations of historians accepted Burns' work at face value. In dozens of books and articles, historians have generalized from a homogenized parochial educational experience developed by Burns in his books.

But the recent generation of historians of American Catholicism has cast a skeptical eye on the two Burns volumes and on other works based on his thesis. "Now a generation is on the scene," notes Martin Marty, "one that is impatient with a mere address to the old questions . . . . [They] bring this process to a new stage precisely by examining the walls of the old ghettos as well as the fissures in them. Here is no church history that sees the church protected as if lead-encased in a hostile environment but, instead, the story of people in the incipient pluralism of an expanding metropolis."[21] Marty rightly credits Jay P. Dolan of the University of Notre Dame with a major

---

21. Martin E. Marty, "Foreword," in Dolan, Immigrant Church, p. ix.

portion of the responsibility for "de-ghettoizing" American Catholic history.

The educational differences from one diocese to another underscore the central fact that the American Church has always been very much of a human organization, one fraught with the difficulties of establishing itself in a democratic society. Different educational problems and circumstances elicited different responses from one diocese to the next depending on the nature of relations between Catholics and non-Catholics and between different groups within the Catholic community itself. The chapters that follow show how the dioceses of Chicago and Milwaukee fit into the rich mosaic that is the history of Catholic education in nineteenth century urban America.

CHAPTER I

CATHOLIC SOCIAL INSTITUTIONS AND URBAN DEVELOPMENT

I

The Catholic Church, like many religious denominations, committed itself to the improvement of American life by establishing a variety of urban social institutions. Hospitals, asylums, colleges and schools were obvious improvements to the urban landscape and each of these social institutions helped Catholics and some non-Catholics to cope with city life. The formation of Church-sponsored organizations such as the St. Vincent de Paul Society and the Irish Colonization Society also gave direction to Catholic concern about urban problems.[1] Even non-Catholics appreciated the value of the Church's work in American cities.

The impact of the Church's efforts, however, varied from one city to the next. In Boston and New York, for example, Catholic institutions served immigrants almost exclusively. Protestant benevolent associations and municipal law had established hospitals, schools, and asylums long before the arrival of the Church. Boston was committed to public education as early as the seventeenth century and by 1830 also supported asylums for orphans and the indigent. New York was similarly committed to social wel-

---

1. Robert D. Cross, "The Changing Image of the City Among American Catholics," Catholic Historical Review, 48 (April 1962): 33-53; Jay P. Dolan, The Immigrant Church: New York's Irish and German Catholics, 1815-1865 (Baltimore, 1975).

fare. In fact, the efforts of New York's citizens were so extensive that Charles Dickens acknowledged the fact during his visit
to the city in 1842. When the Catholic Church began to grow in
Boston and New York in the 1830s and 1840s, there was no role for
Catholic hospitals, asylums, or schools outside the confines of
the immigrant neighborhood. There were occasional exceptions, of
course. Some Boston and New York elites, for example, were fond
of giving their daughters a convent education. For the most
part, however, the native population in these cities was obliv-
ious to Catholic social institutions.[2]

The Catholic experience in the upper Midwest was different.
When the Church came to Chicago and Milwaukee in the 1840s, these
small towns had only a few public institutions and these were
badly overcrowded. It is not surprising, therefore, that the establishment of schools, hospitals, and asylums by the Church had
an impact on both the Catholic and the non-Catholic populations.
These institutions frequently operated in public capacities and
received funding from municipal and state governments for services rendered. Civic leaders and citizens in these cities

---

2. For details on Boston, see Oscar Handlin, Boston's
Immigrants (Cambridge, 1941), pp. 119, 162; Roger Lane, Policing
the City (Cambridge, 1967), pp. 16-20; Nathan I. Huggins,
Protestants Against Poverty (Westport, CT, 1971); Donna Merwick,
Boston Priests, 1848-1911 (Cambridge, 1973), pp. 12-61. For
details on New York, see Bayard Still, ed., Mirror for Gotham
(New York, 1956), pp. 124, 136; George Jacoby, Catholic Child
Care in Nineteenth Century New York (Washington, DC, 1941),
pp. 3-86; Carl F. Kaestle, The Evolution of an Urban School
System: New York City, 1750-1850 (Cambridge, 1974), pp. 80-111,
164-169, 185-191; Dolan, Immigrant Church, pp. 11-26, 121-140.

naturally applauded these efforts of the Church because such assistance was in the best interest of their communities.[3]

These initial establishments were used by non-Catholics for only a short time, however. Other denominations quickly established social institutions of their own in the years after 1850. Yet the influential role played by these Catholic hospitals, schools, and asylums in the development of Chicago and Milwaukee dramatized the difference between the Catholic experience in the East and that in the Middle West.

II

Chicago was a city of dreams in the 1830s, years of immense speculation and hope. "Almost every person I met," wrote one visitor in 1833, "regarded Chicago as the germ of an immense city and speculators have already bought up at high prices all the building ground in the neighborhood."[4] Many Chicagoans personally exuded the confidence so essential to the growth of their city. "At fourteen I fancied I could do anything," boasted William B. Ogden, the first mayor of Chicago, "and that nothing

---

3. This point is argued most persuasively by Daniel Boorstin in The Americans: The National Experience (New York, 1965), pp. 113-169. Also see Bayard Still, "Patterns of Mid-Nineteenth Century Urbanization in the Middle West," in Alexander B. Callow, ed., American Urban History (New York, 1969), pp. 112-125; and Stanley Elkins and Eric McKitrick, "A Meaning for Turner's Frontier: Democracy in the Old Northwest," Political Science Quarterly 69 (September 1954): 348.

4. Patrick Shireff, A Tour of North America (Edinburgh, 1835), as reprinted in Bessie L. Pierce, ed., As Others See Chicago (Chicago, 1933), p. 66. For the general history of Chicago in the 1840s, see Bessie L. Pierce, A History of Chicago (3 vols., New York, 1937), vol. 1.

was impossible, and ever since I have been trying to prove it with some success."[5]   But Chicago's great potential seemed to wither with the national financial depression of 1837.   The dreams of the mid-thirties melted into the "blight and mildew" of the early forties.

Increasingly during the 1840s, city officials looked for ways to make their city a decent place to live.   They had made some progress before the panic by establishing an almshouse in a building with the city jail, the records office, and the fire engine company.   But these facilities were woefully inadequate and complaints began to appear regularly in the press.   Mayor Ogden's rudimentary police force could not contend with Chicago's crime rate which, at times, rivaled that of a California mining camp. With no hospital and few doctors, health care suffered.[6]   The county almshouse provided only emergency care for the increasing number of homeless children whose parents were the victims of the high mortality rate.   Even though the city council had supported elementary education since the early 1830s, both the number of schools and the quality of the instruction were inadequate.[7]   An

5. Boorstin, The Americans, p. 116.

6. Harold M. Mayer and Richard C. Wade, Chicago: Growth of a Metropolis (Chicago, 1969), p. 76; Pierce, History of Chicago, 1:216-217, 255.   Health care in Chicago was extremely irregular before 1850.   There is evidence that the city council authorized a public hospital in 1846, but there is little evidence that the institution was ever opened.   A homeopathic hospital was opened in 1849, but it was boycotted by the medical profession; see James Brown, The History of Public Assistance in Chicago, 1833-1893 (Chicago, 1941), pp. 3-5, 16-37.

7. Edwin Gale, Reminiscences of Early Chicago and Vicinity (Chicago, 1902), p. 220.

ever-increasing influx of new residents caused Ogden and other city leaders to despair about finding the money or the personnel to solve Chicago's social problems.

Central to the city's dilemma was the impoverished state of its new residents, many of whom were Catholic immigrants from Ireland and Germany. One city directory noted that there were 2,000 Catholics in Chicago by the early 1840s. Such a rapid growth from a single small parish ten years earlier encouraged the American bishops to recommend that Chicago be made a diocese. In 1843, the bishops recommended and the Pope selected William Quarter, an Irish priest from New York, to serve as the first bishop.

Quarter was proud of his appointment and eager to build his diocese. Moreover, he was very pleased by the reception he received upon his arrival in May, 1844. "I am very happy to inform you," he wrote to Archbishop Richard Purcell of Cincinnati, "that a spirit of great liberality exists toward Catholics in this state, and a word exasperating or painful to Catholics, I have never heard uttered. Indeed, the citizens appear all like the members of one united and well-organized family where each one consults for the benefit and advantage of all."[8] Quarter was probably exaggerating, but cooperation between Catholics and

---

8. Quarter to Purcell, September 2, 1844, UNDA; Quarter to "Father Carroll" of St. Louis University, July 30, 1844, St. Louis University Archives (hereinafter cited as SLUA). Information on Quarter is surveyed in Gilbert H. Garraghan, The Catholic Church in Chicago, 1837-1871 (Chicago, 1922). For a general history of Catholic education in Chicago, see James W. Sanders, The Education of an Urban Minority: Catholics in Chicago, 1833-1965 (New York, 1977).

other Chicagoans did provide the city with a number of social institutions.

The first cooperative effort was the University of St. Mary of the Lake. In the years before public higher education, the Illinois State Assembly granted tax free charters to denominationally affiliated colleges and universities. In exchange for this privilege, the denomination was to open its institution to all students regardless of religious persuasion. Quarter agreed to this provision and on December 23, 1844, the legislature granted a charter for the establishment of a new Catholic university. Even though the legislative action was not extraordinary, the bishop was elated. "The Protestants show the greatest kindness and liberality," Quarter exclaimed in one letter. "I mean to improve it <u>while I have a chance</u>."[9]

In April 1845, a group of non-Catholics made a contribution to the bishop in the form of a grant of land on which to locate the new college. Mayor Ogden and his colleagues realized that a university would not only add to the prestige of the city, but also would increase property values in the area.[10] As major real estate speculators, these men stood to gain handsomely by locating the university near their property. It was an arrangement that benefitted everyone. Quarter received the property he

---

9. Quarter to John Hughes, December 25, 1844 (italics in original); copy in the Archives of the Archdiocese of Chicago (hereinafter cited as AAC); Act of Incorporation of the University of St. Mary of the Lake by the Illinois General Assembly, December 23, 1844, copy in AAC.

10. The deed for the Lake Street property, dated April 13, 1845, bearing the signatures of William B. Ogden, Walter L. Newberry and others, is in AAC.

needed for his university and Ogden and his colleagues had an investment in the future growth of the city.

Turning his attention to other community projects, Quarter welcomed the Sisters of Mercy to Chicago in 1846 and by 1852, the small band of sisters had established five schools, two orphan asylums, a hospital, and an academy.[11] The first of these projects was St. Xavier's Female Seminary, a secondary school for the daughters of Chicago's elite. The institution successfully attracted the daughters of both Protestant and Catholic families. In fact, several alumnae remembered a majority of the students being Protestants.[12] St. Xavier's offered exactly the kind of refined, genteel, convent education that some upper class Protestant parents wanted for their daughters. The sisters, for their part, encouraged this ecumenical trend by excusing non-Catholic students from all religious instruction. Once again the relationship between Catholics and non-Catholics proved to be mutually beneficial. The sisters had a prosperous select school which provided income to support other programs and a number of

11. Quarter to the Leopoldine Association in Vienna, December 13, 1845, AAC; Quarter to the Society for the Propagation of the Faith, Lyon, France, May 29, 1845, and December 7, 1846, copies in AAC; no adequate history of the order has been written, but the story can be pieced together from parish histories and memoirs; see James J. Thompson, Antecedents of the Archdiocese of Chicago (Chicago, 1921), pp. 698-702; M. Gabriel O'Brien, Reminiscences of Seventy Years (Chicago, 1916); Garraghan, Catholic Church in Chicago, pp. 150-163.

12. Bedilia K. Garraghen, "Reminiscences," Illinois Catholic Historical Review, 2 (January 1920): 265-267; Harriet Randolph Rosa, "Memoirs," Rosa Collection, Chicago Historical Society (hereinafter cited as CHS); Sister Mary Agatha O'Brien to the Society for the Propagation of the Faith, December 4, 1847, copy in AAC; Chicago Daily Democrat, October 24, 1846.

non-Catholics had the kind of education they wanted for their daughters.

The sisters continued to work in secondary education, but their momentum was interrupted by the sudden death of Bishop Quarter in 1848 and a growing tension between Catholics and non-Catholics. Although city leaders such as William Ogden, Walter Newberry, and J. Young Scammon attended Quarter's funeral, many Chicagoans were beginning to feel uneasy about the growing numbers of Catholics immigrating to their city. Some Protestant ministers played on this fear and warned their flocks of the "power of Rome." They cautioned all who would listen to be wary of Catholic assistance. One denominational paper went so far as to claim that any Protestant who converted to Catholicism was either "criminal or crazy."[13]

Chicagoans generally were confused about Catholicism. On the one hand they had read the shocking tales of Maria Monk's life in a Montreal convent and heard the rumors about an invasion of the Jesuits in the Middle West. On the other hand, Chicagoans knew many Catholics such as Bishop Quarter and the Sisters of Mercy who were genuine assets to the city. Overall, non-Catholic Chicagoans seemed to reject Catholicism as an abstract religion, but accept the social institutions established by Catholics in their city.[14]

---

13. Western Herald, September 9, 1846; Pierce, History of Chicago, 1:232-233.

14. John P. Senning, "The Know Nothing Party in Illinois," Journal of the Illinois State Historical Society, 7 (1914): 7-33; see also, Thomas P. O'Keefe, "Chicago's Flirtation with Political Nativism," Records of the American Catholic Historical Society,

Quarter's successor was a Belgian Jesuit named James O. Van de Velde. Somewhat of an intellectual, Van de Velde spoke five languages and was president of St. Louis University before his consecration as bishop. Upon his arrival in Chicago, he urged the Sisters of Mercy to expand the educational and social services that they had started under Bishop Quarter. With this encouragement, the sisters established two free schools for Catholic children, a night school for adults and an employment agency, and a boarding house for working women.[15]

The cholera epidemic of 1849 emphasized the need for better health care and the nuns agreed to open and staff a hospital with the assistance of the city's physicians. The Illinois Hospital of the Lakes, later Mercy Hospital, opened in 1851. "Patients of all religious denominations are admitted without distinction," proclaimed one early announcement, "and every effort is afforded them to be visited by the ministers of their respective persuasions."[16]

The epidemic also left the city with many orphans, and the sisters responded to their needs as well. Van de Velde recorded that a new asylum was in operation by August 1849, in the midst of the epidemic. Money for the construction of a permanent fa-

---

82 (September 1971); for a picture of the hostility toward Catholics in the East, see Vincent P. Lannie, Public Money and Parochial Education (Cleveland, 1968); Kaestle, Evolution of an Urban School System; Handlin, Boston's Immigrants, pp. 178-206; Ray A. Billington, The Protestant Crusade, 1800-1860 (New York, 1938).

15. Thompson, Antecedents of the Archdiocese of Chicago, pp. 698-699.

16. Western Tablet, February 28, 1852.

cility was a problem; two collections in the autumn of that year had depleted available funds in the city. On October 16, Van de Velde met with Illinois Governor Augustus C. French to petition for aid for the orphans. In December the bishop sponsored a concert to raise money and sent Walter Quarter, brother of the late bishop, to raise funds from among the Catholics in eastern dioceses. Finally in October 1850, Van de Velde had the funds needed to construct a permanent asylum building.[17]

The asylum, along with the university, the academies, the schools, and the hospital represented the Catholic contributions toward the improvement of Chicago life in the 1840s. "It has required no small amount of energy and means to accomplish this," wrote Van de Velde, "thus enriching our city with evidence of the philanthropy of its citizens."[18] The influence and visibility of these Catholic social institutions reached their peak in the early 1850s.

Protestants established voluntary associations to distribute food and clothing to the indigent, but they built few institutions of their own before 1850 because they lacked the necessary funds and people to support them. After 1850, however, Protestants became more active in the social welfare of Chicago and the relative importance of Catholic social institutions began to decline. Two new medical colleges with hospital facilities made the city less dependent on Mercy Hospital. The Chicago

17. "Dairy of James O. Van de Velde," original in AAC, also published in Souvenir of the Silver Jubilee in the Episcopacy of Patrick A. Feehan (Chicago, 1891), pp. 110-115, 134-135.

18. Ibid., p. 133.

Lyceum and the Young Men's Christian Association offered programs in adult education and other social services. The Chicago Orphan Asylum and Reform School opened in 1855 giving non-Catholics another option for the care of dependent children.[19]

There also were other reasons for the declining importance of Catholic social institutions. One simple reason was that the Church was unable to build enough social institutions to keep pace with the rapid growth of the city. Catholic hospitals, asylums, and schools served proportionally smaller percentages of the population after 1850 than in the 1840s. Another reason for the decline was the turmoil brought on by the growth of nativism. Even though the Know Nothing Party never gained much strength in Chicago, the tension precipitated by the party in other regions of the country caused some distrust of Catholics even in Chicago. There is no question that nativism affected the willingness of some non-Catholics to use Catholic social institutions.[20]

All this is not to say that Catholic institutions ceased to make an impression on non-Catholics in Chicago after 1850. In 1856, for example, the Sisters of the Holy Cross founded an industrial school for girls of all religious denominations. In 1859, the bishop established the House of the Good Shepherd for delinquent women and the institution received a stipend from the city for its work.[21] The Alexian Brothers Hospital and the Angel

---

19. Pierce, History of Chicago, 2:443.

20. Senning, "Know Nothing Movement in Illinois," pp. 7-33; O'Keefe, "Flirtation with Nativism."

21. Pierce, History of Chicago, 2:443.

Guardian Orphanage came into existence in 1865. Father Patrick
Dunne founded an industrial school for boys in the mid-1860s, and
the university was re-established at the same time. For all of
these efforts, the daily newspapers acknowledged the good work of
the Catholic Church.[22]

Calamity and crisis also underscored the importance of
Catholic social institutions. The devastation of the city by
fire in 1871 precipitated a tremendous immediate need for social
services and institutions of all types and kinds. The Church
managed to rebuild those institutions lost in the fire and also
to build new hospitals, asylums, and schools throughout the 1870s
and 1880s. In August 1872, the newly founded St. Joseph's hospital, and the attending Sisters of Charity received the thanks of
the Tribune editors for the sisters' work on behalf of the most
pitiful dependents in the city.[23] Other religious orders were
responsible for homes for the aged, orphan asylums, and a kinder-
garten for the children of working mothers.[24] Additional asylums
and hospitals were constructed in the 1880s.[25]

It was the specialized educational efforts of the Church
which received the attention of the press in the 1870s and 1880s.
Both the Chicago Tribune and the Chicago Times supported public
education, but where these institutions failed, these papers ac-

---

22. Chicago Tribune, January 28, 1864.

23. Ibid., August 21, 1872, August 30, 1873, August 26, 1881;
Chicago Times, June 4, 1877.

24. Pierce, History of Chicago, 3:447.

25. Ibid., Thompson, Antecedents of the Archdiocese of
Chicago, p. 747.

knowledged the work of the Catholic Church. During the 1870s, the total enrollment in the city's public secondary schools ranged between 600 and 1,000 students and few of these were females. Thus the press praised the Catholic female academies for conducting "a high standard of education with thorough methods, perfect discipline, and teachers of the highest quali-fication."[26]

In an another area -- industrial education -- the public school system was completely remiss, much to the dismay of the press.[27] When the Church established the Chicago Industrial School for Girls in 1877 and St. Mary's Training School for Boys in 1882, the Tribune applauded the schools. "St. Mary's has a wide field of usefulness," went the editorial. "Its purpose is admirable, its projectors are worthy the thanks of the whole com-munity, and it should have a generous, hearty, sustained sup-port."[28] The City Council agreed and used these schools for the care of wards of the courts.

The involvement of Catholicism and Catholics in the urban affairs of Chicago was extensive and that involvement came at the most advantageous time in the city's history. The assets of the Church -- especially her social institutions -- were welcome ad-ditions to the urban landscape and often these institutions were the first of their kind in Chicago. In addition, Catholics in

---

26. Chicago Times, June 4, 1877; Chicago Tribune, June 26, 1874, September 14, 1858; Chicago Daily Journal, August 5, 1879.

27. Chicago Tribune, May 1, 15, June 5, 1881.

28. Ibid., June 18, October 9, 1882.

Chicago were very involved in the life of their city, as involved as any other denomination. "It is a city," claimed one Catholic from Chicago, "where the general community is liberal and comparatively without prejudice, where the press will truthfully report and discuss our affairs with fairness."[29]

III

The impact of Catholic social institutions in Milwaukee was similar to that in Chicago. Indeed, during the formative decade of the 1840s, the two cities were remarkably alike. As Chicago's sister city, Milwaukee experienced the same rapid growth and faced the same problems in providing urban services.[30] During the 1830s, Milwaukee was no more than a fur-trading village of Indians and trappers. Like Chicago, Milwaukee was a city of dreams, and even the depression of 1837 did little to dampen the spirit. The rich farmlands to the west of the city and her natural harbor made Milwaukee the center of commerce for the Wisconsin Territory.[31]

The opportunities for employment attracted a large body of newcomers to Milwaukee, and its population increased from 1,700 citizens in 1840 to over 20,000 in 1850. The largest group was the foreign-born, which by 1850 constituted sixty-four percent of the population. The rapid growth in the population buoyed the optimism of civic leaders. "The tide of emigration to the West

---

29. Ibid., May 12, 1881.

30. Bayard Still, Milwaukee (Madison, WI, 1948), pp. 96-108.

31. Ibid., p. 52.

seems to increase daily," wrote one Milwaukee editor, ". . . what an enterprising spirit characterizes the American people . . . . In no other country have towns and villages sprung up so suddenly as this. Everything seems to go ahead with railroad velocity."[32] At the same time, Milwaukee retained a small town flavor. "Everybody is interested in his neighbors circumstances, his family affairs and religious convictions," wrote Bishop John Henni as late as 1851, "and strives to become acquainted with them."[33]

Native Milwaukeeans greeted this wave of new residents with mixed feelings.[34] Even though new citizens meant further growth and prosperity, the size of the immigrant population was so overwhelming as to make the city seem foreign.[35] Even though visible evidence of native resentment was infrequent, it nevertheless existed. On Thanksgiving Day 1844, for example, a Congregationalist minister attacked "immoral aliens" who lacked the integrity and discretion to be good citizens because they were controlled by an "immoral" clergy.[36] A conciliatory rebuttal by Bishop Henni stopped the incident from spreading, but anti-ethnic

32. Milwaukee Sentinel, May 26, 1845.

33. Henni to the Archbishop of Vienna, January 14, 1851, in the Archives of St. Francis Seminary, St. Francis, Wisconsin (hereinafter cited as ASFS).

34. William George Bruce, "Memoirs of William George Bruce," Wisconsin Magazine of History 16 (June 1933): 362.

35. Henni to the Archbishop of Vienna, January 14, 1851, ASFS.

36. J. J. Miter, The Patriot's Duty (Milwaukee, 1845), pp. 13-18; Milwaukee Sentinel January 29, 1845; Peter L. Johnson, The Crosier on the Frontier (Madison, WI, 1959), pp. 79-80; Rudolf Koss, Milwaukee (Milwaukee, 1871), p. 196.

and anti-Catholic feelings never abated completely. Generally,
native Milwaukeeans respected the rights of immigrants and
Henni's ability as a community leader won him the respect of the
city's political leadership.[37]

The rapid growth of Milwaukee during the forties also caused
other problems. Like Chicago, Milwaukee had a difficult time
meeting the demand for urban services. One of the biggest problems was schooling; throughout the nineteenth century, private
schools educated a substantial percentage of the city's children.
In 1845, for example, there were thirteen schools in the city;
nine of them were private and only one third of the children
between the ages of five and twenty attended any school at all.
Even though the city established a school board in 1846, it
failed to increase taxes to finance additional schools.[38]

The school board was not the only organization in Milwaukee
without money in the 1840s. When the Vatican established the
Diocese of Milwaukee in November 1843, its legacy was composed
only of faith and hope; the charity had to come from other
sources. But the appointment of John Martin Henni as bishop
brought to Milwaukee one of the most active fund raisers in the
nineteenth century Church. Before his appointment as bishop, the
Swiss-born Henni had been a priest in Cincinnati where he
established a number of German parishes as well as the city's
first German Catholic newspaper. The new bishop brought two

---

37. Kathleen Neils Conzen, Immigrant Milwaukee, 1836-1860:
Accommodation and Community in a Frontier City (Cambridge, 1976).

38. Laurence Larson, A Financial History of Milwaukee
(Madison, WI, 1908), pp. 42-43; Conzen, Immigrant Milwaukee.

priests with him to Milwaukee -- Josef Salzmann, Henni's chief fund raiser, and Michael Heiss, Henni's protege and eventual successor as archbishop. Along with Martin Kundig, an old school friend who became Henni's vicar general, these men grappled with the poverty of their new diocese.[39]

Poverty did not dampen the bishop's determination to make whatever improvements were mutually beneficial to the life of their adopted city. After persuading the Sisters of Charity to come to Milwaukee, Henni established two schools under their care -- one located in the basement of St. Peter's Church and the other in the sisters' convent. The bishop loaned the basement school at St. Peter's to the city for use as the First Ward Public School. The Sentinel noted that the space was "kindly placed at the disposal of the commissioners," and thanked the bishop for its use.[40]

It was, however, the female academy conducted at the sisters' residence which attracted the attention of a number of non-Catholics. The policy of optional religious instruction, the wide-ranging curriculum, and the general reputation of the sisters as superior teachers attracted many Protestant girls.

---

39. Information on Henni can be found in Peter L. Johnson, Crosier on the Frontier; on Kundig in Peter L. Johnson in Stuffed Saddlebags (Milwaukee, 1942); on Heiss in M. Mileta Ludwig, Right Hand Glove Uplifted (New York, 1970); on Salzmann in Joseph Ranier, A Noble Priest: Josef Salzmann (Milwaukee, 1903). Michael Heiss to Killian Kleiner, April 29, 1850, ASFS, printed in Salesianum 19 (1914): 8.

40. Milwaukee Sentinel, September 12, 1846; Daniel O'Hearn, Fifty Years at St. John's Cathedral, 1847-1897 (Milwaukee, 1897), p. 170.

"Hardly a day passes," wrote Henni, "when Protestant parents do not bring their daughters to the academy."[41]

Not everyone was happy with this ecumenical approach to education. One denominational paper aptly summarized the attitude of many Protestant parents toward this school: "Protestant families are beguiled by the great flourish of schools taught by the Sisters of Charity, and place their children under their care. When remonstrated, they tell us: 'Oh, it is a very good school -- the teachers do not introduce religious tenets -- the pupil is left entirely free choice.'"[42] The article reflected the widespread concern among the Protestant clergy about this educational phenomenon. The matter was serious enough for Protestant ministers to warn their congregations about the "dangers" of a convent education.

When Henni invited the Sisters of Charity to Wisconsin, he asked them to start a hospital as well as the schools, "and before all, asylums for poor orphans."[43] But the asylums, one for boys and one for girls, were not established until 1849, and with the cholera epidemic of that year, they were filled to capacity almost immediately.

The hospital emerged under the same crisis conditions. The perpetuation of cholera and small pox convinced the city council

---

41. Mother Etienne Hall, 1845-1855 (Emmitsburg, MD, 1939), 15-16; Peter L. Johnson, Daughters of Charity, 1846-1946 (Milwaukee, 1946), p. 19.

42. Western Herald, September 9, 1846.

43. Henni to Mother Xavier of the Sisters of Charity, Emmitsburg, Md., January 1, 1845, cited in O'Hearn, Fifty Years, p. 34.

that public measures were necessary to protect the health of the citizenry. In 1846, they required the vaccination of all citizens for smallpox, but this failed to terminate the disease. The Sentinel encouraged the city to construct a hospital as the first line of defense, and in May 1848, the Sisters of Charity established the first infirmary in the city with the approval of the city council.[44]

The relationship between the hospital and various urban groups was amicable. When the hospital first opened, the sisters made an appeal to the populace through the press. "Lacking the means to procure the necessary outfit of furniture and so on," went the article, "the Sisters appeal to your charity for aid. The institution will be open to all citizens or strangers without distinction of class, religion or nation."[45] The sisters also advertised a policy of religious freedom and toleration by incorporating these principles into the rules of the institution. "The right of conscience," they noted, "must be held paramount to all others."[46]

The Milwaukee City Medical Association granted its approval to the hospital and doctors from all sections of the city joined the staff. The sisters also cared for the mentally ill and received a stipend from the city for these services. In 1850, the

---

44. Milwaukee Sentinel, May 7, 1849; Johnson, Daughters of Charity, pp. 36-45.

45. Manuscript dated February 2, 1848, in St. Mary's Hospital Archives, Milwaukee, cited in Johnson, Daughters of Charity, p. 38.

46. Catholic Almanac (1849) cited in Johnson, Daughters of Charity, p. 39.

sisters were the principal agency for health care in Milwaukee and at the request of Mayor D. A. J. Upham, they established a second hospital for incoming immigrants.

By 1850, Milwaukee had overcome the hard times of first settlement. With the assistance of the Sisters of Charity, the city was providing care for the indigent, the dependent, the sick, and the insane. In addition, Catholic schools relieved some of the pressure on the public schools. In the 1840s, Milwaukee grew from a small town of about 1,700 residents into a city of over 20,000 citizens; the cooperation and involvement of the Catholic Church helped to ease the transition.

After 1850, the impact of Catholic social institutions on the non-Catholic community dropped off sharply, but the reasons for the decline were not quite the same as in Chicago. Even though Milwaukee's population growth continued during the 1850s, it was not as dramatic as Chicago's. The municipal government in Milwaukee in the 1850s was not much better than it had been in the 1840s, and Catholic institutions had little competition. But Milwaukee did experience the ethnic tension which emerged in Chicago. In fact, it was intra-ethnic bitterness, rather than nativism which kept some non-Catholics from patronizing Catholic institutions.

A number of incidents kept tension high during the 1850s. The speaking engagement of a fraudulent "monk", Edward M. Leahy, caused Milwaukee's Irish Catholics to attack the Methodist church where he was lecturing. Even though the incident was defused quickly, it precipitated some ill will among the non-Catholic population.[47] The emigration of large numbers of German atheists

to Milwaukee during the decade led to clashes between religious

and non-religious factions within the city's large German

community.   The "Freethinkers," as the non-religious faction

called itself, "established newspapers and began to agitate

against tax exemptions for church property and published stories

about the "evils" of the Catholic priesthood and convent life.

The bitterness and distrust that resulted from these attacks

undermined some of the positive effects that had been generated

by the establishment of Catholic social institutions.[48]

Perhaps as a reaction to the tension, the Church stepped up

its involvement in urban affairs in the 1850s, especially in the

areas of education, aid to dependent children, and health care.

Such efforts complemented those of the city and helped to improve

relations between Catholics and non-Catholics.[49] Public health

care proved to be the Church's most visible contribution to

Milwaukee life and symbolized time and again Catholic compassion

for all mankind. The gratitude of the city was documented in the

city press. "Amidst scenes often most trying," noted one report,

---

47. Milwaukee Sentinel, April 8, 1851; Ranier, A Noble Priest, pp. 61-62.

48. Ranier, A Noble Priest, 57-59; Johnson, Crosier on the Frontier, 128-129; Heiss to Killian Kleiner, July 6, 1853, ASFS, published in Salesianum, 10 (1914); Wisconsin Banner, November 1, 1852, September 14, 1853; Heiss to Mueller, April 1, 1852, ASFS; Peter M. Abbelen, Venerable Mother M. Caroline Freiss, First Commissary General of the School Sisters of Notre Dame (St. Louis, 1893), 128; Milwaukee Sentinel, September 12, 1855, February 11, 1875.

49. Michael Heiss to Killian Kleiner, July 6, 1853, ASFS, published in Salesianum 10 (1914); Still, Milwaukee, p. 216; Milwaukee Sentinel March 28, 1856.

"did the Sisters of Charity continue their work when Death's daily victims were counted by tens and twenties. The community, grateful and thankful for the noble spirit that knows no color or creed, offered some compensation for the services rendered. The compensation was respectfully declined."[50] A second cholera epidemic in 1856 hit Milwaukee very hard, and once again the sisters were there to help.

The city fathers did not forget this community spirit even after the cholera epidemic had passed. In 1856, the city council donated three acres of public land to the Sisters of Charity for the construction of a new hospital. In 1859, the city council designated the newly-opened St. Mary's hospital as the caretaker of all the county sick, and fiscal appropriations were made for those services throughout the 1860s.

The state used the institution for the care of wounded veterans of the Civil War because a delegation from the state legislature had found "excellent management in every department of the hospital."[51] The Sentinel added that "through the untiring and unselfish devotion of the Sisters and the benevolence of Milwaukeeans -- Protestant and Catholic alike -- it has grown to its present capacity of usefulness."[52] Henni was pleased with the relationship and noted that "the charitable spirit of Catholics has won the admiration of Protestants for our religion

---

50. Milwaukee Sentinel, October 22, 1856, April 27, 1855, July 31, 1854, August 8, 1864.

51. Johnson, Daughters of Charity, pp. 72-73, 92-93.

52. Milwaukee Sentinel, August 8, 1864.

and endeavors.   I found that well-to-do Protestants were the outstanding benefactors of this fine institution who, because of their own serious denominational differences, could not accomplish anything similar."[53]

Aid to dependent children was another service in which the Church and the state combined their efforts.   The rapid rise in the number of dependent children caused by the Civil War and the tragic sinking of the steamboat Lady Elgin in 1860 dramatized the need for a municipal system of care for the unfortunate.   The professionalism of the two Catholic asylums run by the Sisters of Charity was a matter of record and the state legislature sought the cooperation of the sisters in caring for the rising number of orphans.   A Sentinel reporter who visited the orphanage in 1859 wrote that the girls' asylum was "a labor of love . . . performed under the immediate eye and supervision of those who have made it their mission."[54]

The Sentinel took a special interest in Catholic asylum care, in part because there were no public facilities.   Visits to the girls' asylum in 1862 and 1872 merited praise for the Sisters of Charity in general and the asylum in particular.[55]   The gratitude extended to the sisters was reinforced by the addition of asylums for the elderly and for foundlings.   "There are none but will be gratified," wrote one Sentinel reporter, "to learn of the

53. Henni to Archbishop Reisach of Munich, March 26, 1859, ASFS.

54. Milwaukee Sentinel, October 14, 1859.

55. Ibid., February 10, 1865, November 4, 1872; Johnson, Daughters of Charity, pp. 148-149, 151-161.

progress of this good work. All are prepared to aid the patient toilers who have been willing to give up their lives for the benefit of the enfeebled, asking no compensation other than the sweet consciousness of knowing that they are doing a useful work."[56]

Certainly the establishment of hospitals, asylums, and schools earned the appreciation of Milwaukeeans throughout the nineteenth century. Milwaukee in 1840 was a town without much of a past, but with a very optimistic future; the Catholic Church and her followers helped to make the future even brighter. Perhaps the attitude of Milwaukee Catholics toward community affairs was best symbolized in the name of their paper, The Catholic Citizen, for Catholics did see themselves as citizens with an active concern for the quality of life in Milwaukee.

IV

The differences between the Catholic experience in Boston and New York and in Chicago and Milwaukee calls attention to the subtle relationship between the church and the city. At the very least, the Catholic experience in these two midwestern cities forces historians to adjust their portrait of nineteenth century Catholicism as little more than a ghettoized victim of American nativism. Beyond this assessment, the two midwestern experiences highlight the extent to which the Catholic influence and involvement in specific cities was determined by the accidents of

56. Milwaukee Daily News, April 28, 1876; Milwaukee Sentinel, June 9, 1877; Johnson, Daughters of Charity, pp. 196-197.

local urban development. When the Catholic Church began to develop in Boston and New York in the 1840s, adequate social institutions were already in operation. With a Protestant tradition in hospital and asylum care, there was no city-wide role for the institutional Church. It provided for its own followers and that was the extent of its involvement.

But the newness of Chicago and Milwaukee and their drastic need for social institutions and leadership precipitated a different kind of experience for the Catholic Church in the upper Middle West. The Church mobilized quickly and offered these cities needed hospitals, asylums, and schools. Non-Catholic leaders in Chicago and Milwaukee accepted these institutions with gratitude because they made their cities more attractive and helped to insure future growth.[57] The continued growth of the immigrant and Catholic communities allowed Catholic laymen to participate in community affairs to an extent not achieved in the east.

---

57. Sam B. Warner and Colin B. Burke, "Cultural Change and the Ghetto," Journal of Contemporary History 4 (1969): 173-187.

CHAPTER II

THE CHURCH-STATE-SCHOOL ISSUE

I

The Catholic Church played an active role in the development of Chicago and Milwaukee through the establishment of hospitals, asylums, schools, and other social institutions. The
Church contributed substantially to the quality of life in those
cities and earned the gratitude of citizens regardless of denominational affiliation. Catholics, in turn, were optimistic about
their future in these emerging communities. "The character of
the great west and of this city is forming," exclaimed the ebul-
lient editor of the Catholic newspaper in Chicago, "cheerfully
and zealously shall we contribute our influence, whatever it may
be, toward raising that character in a moral point of view to
such a noble elevated position as shall be commensurate with our
future standing in wealth, numbers, and influence."[1] It was a
state of affairs that was significantly different from the
ongoing denominational tension and occasional violence in eastern
dioceses such as Boston, New York, and Philadelphia.

This is not to say that all was peace and harmony between
Catholics and non-Catholics in Chicago and Milwaukee. Indeed,
there were several issues of contention between the two groups

_____

1. Western Tablet, February 28, 1852.

including the issue of the common schools. But such low-level, non-violent social conflict was a normal, even productive, aspect of community decision-making in these developing communities. "If conflict and cooperation seem mutually exclusive and therefore incapable of existing simultaneously," notes Robert R. Dykstra, "we must remember that we are dealing with human behavior which does not always bow to conventional logic . . . . Despite internal agreement on many important themes, each community was a truly pluralistic society with a fairly extensive range of attitudes. Whether townsmen cohered or clashed depended on the degree of concern surrounding particular goals."[2] Dykstra and other scholars point out that social conflict did not necessarily lead to hostility or alienation between opposing factions. In fact, social conflict could even have had a positive impact on urban development by helping the community to better define its goals.

II

So it was in Chicago when Catholics and non-Catholics clashed over education. Throughout the nineteenth century, the two groups argued the merits and demerits of common public schools versus private, church-sponsored institutions. Was it constitutional to tax citizens for the support of schools they found offensive? Did the state have the right to control the language and content of parochial schools? Catholics in Chicago

---

2. Robert R. Dykstra, The Cattle Towns (New York, 1968), p. 365.

said "no" to both questions. Exercising their rights as citizens, they vigorously argued their position in the press, before the state assembly, at state constitutional conventions, and at the ballot box. Catholics never lost faith in the righteousness of their cause.

At the center of this seemingly endless debate was the role of the state versus the role of the church in the education of children. Even though tax-supported schools existed in Chicago as early as 1833, most children who attended school were privately educated. But beginning in the early 1850s, public-spirited citizens in Chicago campaigned for a well-funded system of common schools to replace the patchwork of private institutions.

Although most citizens supported the measure, the Church stood in visible opposition. Believing that daily denominational instruction should be a vital part of the curriculum, Catholics could hardly support the idea of common schools. Instead, they proposed that each denomination be given a share of the state school fund for the support of private, church-operated institutions.

Over the next four decades, Catholics and non-Catholics debated the church-state-school issue. A final resolution was never achieved; in fact, the issue is still being debated today. Yet through dialogue, the two sides shaped the content of the public school curriculum and defined the rights of Catholic citizens to establish and control their own private schools. It was a significant accomplishment that has ramifications even to the present day.

There was no dramatic event that marked the beginning of the debate on education in Chicago. Schooling gradually became a major public issue between 1848 and 1855 as various civic groups rallied behind the campaign for tax-supported common schools. Catholics were conspicuous by their absence from the campaign and were criticized for their lack of community spirit.[3] Most Chicagoans were hopeful, however, that the Church would eventually change its position and join the campaign for common schools.

The debate reached a new level in 1855 when an act introduced in the Illinois General Assembly proposed that the state provide financial support for all public schools. The new law created a real estate property tax to be used to generate school funds. Private schools could not receive aid unless they submitted to the control of public school officials. Even though few private schools had ever received private aid in the past, the new law closed off the possibility of it ever happening. Not surprisingly, Chicago Catholics protested the injustice of the bill, but it was a futile campaign. The school bill became law on February 15, 1855.[4]

---

3. The Watchman of the Prairie, April 11, November 14, 1848; Chicago Tribune, April 22, 1853.

4. James Mulligan to Henry Fitch, January 11, 1855, Mulligan Collection, Chicago Historical Society; Laws Passed by the General Assembly of the State of Illinois for the Year 1855 (Springfield, 1856), pp. 51-91.

The question of Catholic rights and public education lay dormant for the next four years. In 1859, the issue reemerged in the public forum because of the treatment of Catholic children in the Chicago Asylum and Reform School. Catholic leaders charged that these impressionable young people were being denied the religious instruction requested by their parents. In August, the Catholic clergy of Chicago petitioned the City Council for a redress of this state of affairs, arguing that the state served as a substitute parent for these children and was obligated to provide proper religious training. The editors of the Chicago Tribune opposed such a notion, arguing that these children should be left free to interpret the Bible "according to its most obvious meaning." The council must have agreed with the Tribune because no action was taken on the petition.[5]

The coming of the Civil War limited the public debate over education. Both Catholics and non-Catholics turned their attention to the preservation of the Union; the press had little time for petty squabbling over schooling. With Chicagoans of all religious faiths fighting against the South, a community spirit reminiscent of the mid 1840s returned to the city. Public school officials emphasized the non-partisan character of their system, and the editors of the Tribune were conciliatory in their comments on Catholicism.[6] Catholic schoolmen avoided controversial

5. Chicago Tribune, June 4, August 26, 1859; Fourth Annual Report of the Chicago Board of Education (Chicago, 1859), p. 3.

6. Eighth Annual Report of the Chicago Board of Education, (Chicago 1863); Chicago Tribune, September 26, 1866, July 7, 1867.

issues and focused on the need for a Catholic reform school and the importance of child-rearing.[7] No one raised the question of dividing the school fund, and certainly this had much to do with the growing religious tolerance during the war and immediately afterwards.[8]

The peace of the 1860s came to an abrupt end with the news that a constitutional convention would convene in Springfield in December 1869. Catholic leaders in Chicago saw the convention as yet another chance to gain a portion of the school fund. Articles appeared in the Catholic press throughout the autumn of 1869 agitating for school tax reform. The Western Catholic, for example, argued that Catholics should receive a share of the school fund so that "the [parochial] schools [can] be made fit for Catholic children."[9] The Catholics marshalled their troops for the convention.

The Tribune summarized the position of the non-Catholic majority. "The duty of the state," observed the Tribune on December 5, "begins and ends when it provides schools which children may attend without any particular theology being thrust at them. If Roman Catholics will not send their children to such schools, but prefer to maintain their own schools, let them do

---

7. "Asylums and Reform Schools for Boys," The Monthly 1 (March 1865): 165-177; Ave Maria 3 (1867): 675-676; Young Catholic Guide 2 (April 1869):179-180.

8. Chicago Tribune, January 7, 1867; June 25, August 2, September 13, 1868; Fourteenth Annual Report of the Chicago Board of Education, (Chicago, 1868), pp. 60-61, 210-215; Fifteenth Annual Report . . . (Chicago, 1869), pp. 46, 191-192.

9. Western Catholic, September 11, October 2, 20, 23, December 4, 1869.

so. The demand of Roman Catholicism to have their schools supported by the state is inadmissible."[10] Public resistance to any
compromise with the Catholic position was firm.

The controversy over the role of religion in education
reached the convention floor on February 12 and again on May 7.
In February, over the protest of Catholic delegates, a majority
of the delegates passed an article prohibiting the distribution
of any state aid to sectarian schools. In May, delegates debated
a proposal to require the use of the Bible in all public schools.
The proposal was controversial because many delegates were concerned about the inconsistency of requiring the use of the Bible,
but prohibiting aid to parochial schools. This second proposal
failed to get the necessary votes, but the Catholic delegates
took small comfort in this victory. The new constitution was
ratified by the convention on July 2 and sent to the populace for
ratification.[11]

The results of the constitutional convention should have resolved the questions about public aid and private education. But
the new constitution seemed to be a preface to continued Catholic
agitation about public education. The convention had raised the
hopes of Catholic leaders that the Church might gain a share of
the school fund and this failure was bitter blow. Their only

---

10. Chicago Tribune, November 11, December 5, 1869; The
Advance, December 23, 1869.

11. Debates and Proceedings of the Constitutional Convention
of the State of Illinois Convened at Springfield, December 13,
1869 (2 vols., Springfield, 1870), pp. 619-620, 623-624, 1760-61,
and 1834; Daniel W. Kucera, Church-State Relationships in
Education in Illinois (Washington, 1955), pp. 87-88.

hope was to find enough votes to reject the new constitution in the general election.

With the vote on the ratification of the constitution a month off, the Tribune exchanged editorials with the Western Catholic over the prerogatives of the state in educational matters. The Western Catholic discussed the differences between its views and those of the Tribune in its issue of June 4, 1870. The Western Catholic maintained that only those citizen who use the public schools should be taxed and that the state had no right to come between parents and their children. The Tribune, of course, disagreed. "To meet the actual or assumed inability and consequent refusal of parents to send their children to school," claimed the Tribune, "the state interferes by the same right that it does to compel parents to properly feed and clothe their children and to provide medical aid when sick . . . . The state has no authority to prohibit other schools nor to compel attendance of children at the public school when they prefer to attend others . . . . Freedom of choice must be left to the parent or guardian, or citizen but the end may be enforced."[12] After the overwhelming approval of the new state constitution on August 8, the matter of dividing the state school fund dropped from the pages of both the Catholic and the secular press.

It would be almost twenty years before Catholics and non-Catholics clashed again over education. During the intervening decades Chicago was made an archdiocese by the Vatican, the num-

---

12. Western Catholic, March 19, June 4, 1870; Chicago Tribune, June 4, 1870.

ber of parochial schools grew from twenty-one to seventy-one, and the enrollment increased from almost 8,500 to over 31,000. This extraordinary growth had come largely from the influx of foreign-born immigrants, the vast majority of whom were Catholic. It was a demographic trend that greatly concerned city and state leaders. Would these new residents adapt to American ways? Could the Catholic Church and its parochial schools be trusted to serve as the primary agents of Americanization? It was non-Catholic doubts such as these that precipitated a major educational controversy in Chicago and Illinois. The question to be addressed was the degree of control the state could and should exercise over private education.

In 1889, the Illinois General Assembly passed an act concerning the education of children known commonly as the "Edwards Law," after its principal proponent, Richard Edwards, the state superintendent of public instruction. The legislation established new regulations on the attendance of children at school. Henceforth, every child between the ages of seven and fourteen was required to attend "some public day school in the city, town, or district in which he resides," for at least sixteen weeks annually. Failure to comply was to be punished by a fine of not less than twenty dollars. "Unlike the previous law which allowed parents to send their children to 'some public or private school,' this new act limited attendance only to the public school."[13] Almost as an afterthought, the General Assembly allowed for attendance at private schools if these institutions

---

13. Kucera, Church-State Relationships, pp. 111-112.

were approved by the local public school board.[14] As if to make certain that their message was clear, the assembly added that "no school shall be regarded as a school under this act unless there shall be taught therein in the English language, reading, arithmetic, history of the United States, and geography."[15]

The act clearly gave the state the right to regulate private education. When the ramifications of the Edwards Law became known, Catholics and Lutherans objected to the power it gave to local school boards and the failure of the law to provide for uniform and objective enforcement.[16] The Catholic bishops of Illinois feared that strict interpretations of the law could easily destroy the rapidly growing system of parochial schools and they protested the legislation. The Tribune, however, saw the Catholic protests as just another veiled attack on the public school system.[17]

Other denominations joined the debate. The Baptists protested against the "hostile attitude" of Lutherans and Catholics toward the public schools. The Congregationalists saw the Catholic-Lutheran protest as "an attack on the common school system." The Methodists objected to any division of the public school fund. None of these Protestant denominations discussed the specific provisions of the Edwards Law. Catholics and

14. Laws Passed by the General Assembly of the State of Illinois for the Year 1869 (Springfield, 1870), p. 237.

15. Ibid.

16. Kucera, Church-State Relationships, p. 113

17. Chicago Tribune, January 14, February 24, 1890.

Lutherans were not objecting to public schooling; they were pro-
testing the right of the state to control parochial education.
In short, Catholics and Lutherans were fighting for the status
quo, not for a change in the laws governing the school fund.[18]

It was inevitable that the antagonism created by the Edwards
Law would reflect itself in the upcoming legislative and guberna-
torial elections. The Republican Party quickly became identified
with the law and Republican papers such as the Tribune were
openly hostile to the Catholic position. The Democrats opposed
the law; they had been critical of the public schools for some
time and they saw the opportunity for political victory by taking
the Catholic-Lutheran position. Rather than defend the law, the
Republicans sought to down play its importance.[19]

But the Democrats would not let the electorate forget the
law or push it aside. "A delegation of German, Lutheran, Catholic, Evangelical, and Reformed laymen and ministers appeared before both the Illinois Democratic and Republican conventions to
demand repeal of the law. The Democrats agreed, pledged to repeal and declared as a self evident truth that 'To determine and
direct the education of children is a natural right of the
parent.' For state superintendent of public instruction, the
Illinois Democrats nominated Henry Raab, a German noted for his

18. Chicago Tribune, November 11, 1890; Minutes of the Meeting
of the Baptist General Association of Illinois 1890; Minutes of
the Annual Meeting of the General Congregational Association of
Illinois, 1890; Minutes of the Illinois Conference of the
Methodist Episcopal Church, 1892, as cited in Kucera, Church-
State Relationships, pp. 117-120.

19. Chicago Tribune, February 25, 1890; Thirty-Fourth Annual
Report of the Chicago Board of Education (Chicago, 1890), p. cvi.

opposition to the Edwards Law. The Illinois Republican convention rebuffed the German committee, although it did promise to
strengthen parental control of education . . . . With a whoop,
they renominated controversial Richard Edwards for superintendent."[20] Never were the Republicans so wrong. Raab defeated
Edwards soundly and the Democrats took control of the lower house
of the General Assembly.[21]

Their election defeat convinced the Republicans that the
Edwards Law was a political albatross. Changes in the law were
necessary if the Lutherans were to return to the Republican
ranks. In the General Assembly, the Republicans quickly proposed
a bill that included all the necessary modifications except for
the clause requiring the use of the English language, but it
failed because the Democrats would not vote for it. Furious over
the bill's defeat, the Republicans accused the Democrats of
blocking passage for political motives. The Democrats countered
with the same charge and a stalemate prevailed.[22]

As the election of 1892 drew closer, both parties did their
best to attract the Lutheran vote. Indeed, the Republicans repu-
diated their previous position and admitted that the Edwards Law
"permits interference with the rights of parents and does give
civil authorities power over private and parochial schools they

---

20. Richard Jensen, The Winning of the Middle West (Chicago,
1972), pp. 134-135.

21. Chicago Tribune, November 7, 8, 1890.

22. Chicago Daily News, June 6, 1891; Chicago Tribune, June
14, 1891.

should not have."[23]   By admitting their mistake, the Republicans hoped to remove the issue from the campaign. As their standard-bearer, they renominated Governor Joseph Fifer.

The Democrats believed that the Edwards Law could be used again to ram home a victory. They nominated John Peter Altgeld, a German-born social and political reformer, who used the school issue as the basis of his campaign. The Democratic paper, The Chicago Times, accused the Republicans of political opportunism and insincerity in their abandonment of the Edwards Law.[24]

The Catholic bishops of Illinois delivered the death blow to the Republicans in September in the form of a joint pastoral letter. The message focused on the injustice of the Edwards Law. "When we consider what we have done and are doing to educate our Catholic children," wrote the bishops, "while we also contribute to the support of the public schools, it seems inexplicable to us that the Legislature of Illinois should have enacted what is known as the Edwards Law; an insidious and unjust law which is really a violation of our most sacred rights as men and citizens . . . . We denounce this law as a violation of our constitutional rights and hold that those who favor it are unworthy of the support of enlightened and fair-minded voters. Let us use all the right and honorable means to have it repealed, and let

23. Chicago Tribune, May 7, 1892.

24. Chicago Times, May 5, August 4, September 14, 1892.

the designing and bigoted be taught that the West is not a field in which their labors will bear fruit."[25]

The Democratic tactics were successful a second time as both the Catholic and the Lutheran vote went solidly for Altgeld. There was no question that the school issue was responsible for Fifer's defeat. One member of the Lutheran school committee put it this way: "I am a Republican and have always voted the party ticket until this time. There was no excuse for bringing the school question in it all. We warned the Republican Party two years ago the question must be settled or it would become an issue in the state campaign of '92."[26] The new General Assembly, overwhelmingly Democratic, quickly repealed the Edwards Law. The new Act Concerning the Education of Children was approved February 17, 1893 and stipulated only that all children between the ages of seven and fourteen must attend some public or private day school for at least sixteen weeks a year.

The elections of 1890 and 1892 marked the end of a forty-year cycle of educational activity in Chicago. Beginning in 1850, public schoolmen attempted to cajole Catholic leaders into supporting public education. For the next four decades the secular press and various school superintendents tried every conceivable argument to accomplish their objective -- a unified common school system for all children.

---

25. Copy in the Archives of the Diocese of Belleville, Illinois as reprinted in Kucera, Church-State Relationships, p. 125.

26. Chicago Tribune, November 10, 1892.

At the same time, using their own press, Catholic leaders did their best to make the public aware of the injustice, inefficiency and inadequacy of the public school system.   They attempted to use the legal and political processes to gain what they believed was just.   These Catholic leaders failed each time.

The cycle was completed when public schoolmen, fearful of the ethnic loyalties of immigrant Catholics, attempted to exert control over parochial education.   The so-called Edwards Law proved a disaster for its supporters and repeal came quickly.   By the mid-1890s, both public and parochial schoolmen were bloodied, but neither group had budged from their positions.

This is not to say that these forty years of argument were without value.   In fact, public schoolmen learned that they had to make their common schools "public" by removing the Bible and other religious books from the curriculum.   Moreover, the constant criticism of public education by Catholic leaders forced schoolmen to be vigilant and meticulous in improving the quality of public instruction.

The criticism of Catholic education by public schoolmen encouraged Catholic leaders to make parochial schools as American as they were Catholic.   "The intelligent and patriotic Catholic citizen," said Judge Thomas Moran, "has reached the conclusion that securing to the rising generation the education that is imported in these schools is the surest guarantee of the permanent preservation of our free institutions.   To preserve civil liberty, a people must have and practice the virtues which exist

only where morality is based on religion."[27] Catholic leaders
took every opportunity to emphasize the commitment of Catholic
education to American values.

III

The social conflict that developed in Milwaukee over the
church-state-school issue was similar in most ways to the
conflict in Chicago. This is not to say that the debates in the
two cities were the same. The most important difference was the
initial involvement of the native population in the fray. In
Chicago, native American common school advocates were at the van-
guard of the debate, meeting each Catholic charge with a rebuttal. In Milwaukee, however, it was two groups of Germans who debated the church-state-school issue. On one side were German
intellectuals -- refugees from the aborted uprisings of 1848 --
who distrusted established religion and favored tax supported
schools. On the other side were German Catholics who were concerned about state intrusions into family matters and worried
about the loss of ethnic identity and religious faith that were
the by-products of a common school education. In short, it was
an intra-ethnic debate with the native American press avoiding
the issue altogether.

Milwaukee's German Catholics saw the schools as a means of
preserving native culture and religious faith. Perhaps the most
articulate statement of that point of view was made by Anthony

---

27. Souvenir of the Silver Jubilee in the Episcopacy of his
Grace, Patrick a. Feehan (Chicago, 1891), p. 340.

Urbanek, a missionary priest, in a letter to the Archbishop of Vienna. "The situation of Catholic schools which insure the future generations is not as good as that of the churches," he wrote. "Catholics, if they wish to preserve their children from Yankeeism are obliged to pay a separate contribution for their own schools . . . . German Catholic schools are the crying need in this country, because German children, if Anglicized, by some strange fate, generally become alienated from Catholic life."[28] Urbanek articulated a general concern among Catholic pastors and parents alike that their children would become devout Catholics only if they remained German-Americans. It was a concern that was both implicit and explicit in the debate over the church-state-school issue in Milwaukee throughout the nineteenth century.

The debate began as something of a family argument. One group of Germans, popularly known as freidinkers (freethinkers), argued against even the slightest cooperation between church and state. In fact, this group went so far as to attack the traditional tax exemption for church property. Writing in newspapers such as the Wisconsin Banner, Volksfreund, Flugbluetter, Humanist, and Atlantis, the freethinkers reflected both atheism and anti-clericalism. "Every honest Catholic is incensed," went one typical editorial in 1852, "by the boundless presumption which several -- only very few we hope -- Catholic priests capture the political freedom of their entire congregations and

_____

28. Peter L. Johnson, ed., "The Letters of the Right Reverend John Martin Henni and the Reverend Anthony Urbanek," Wisconsin Magazine of History, 10 (September 1926): 86-87.

seek to use it as they wish."[29]   The freethinkers saw an evil, priestly plot in the Catholic campaign for a share of the state school fund.

The freethinkers were attacked in the pages of Der Seebote. Even though it was not an official diocesan paper, Der Seebote did carry Catholic news and published the Catholic reaction to the freethinkers.   By March 1853, Der Seebote had launched its own attack.   "When the atheist demands non-religious schools," heralded one editorial, "he claims to act in accordance with his right of freedom of religion . . . .   The atheist says that the state has no right to interfere.   Yet, in reality, he is demanding that the state forbid religion in the schools."[30]   Der Seebote matched the freethinker press salvo for salvo, rallying Catholics to the cause.

The English-speaking Catholic community largely ignored this conflict.   "Here we have four daily English papers in which you can hardly find anything that could be called an attack on the Catholic faith," wrote Michael Heiss with some incredulity in 1853.[31]   In fact, the English language press was positively amicable toward Catholicism.   The editor of the Milwaukee Daily

29. Wisconsin Banner, November 1, 1852, March 23, March 30, April 13, 1853.

30. Der Seebote, March 18, 1853, February 24, 28, March 21, May 12, 1853.

31. Heiss to Killian Kleiner, July 6, 1853, Archives of St. Francis Seminary, St. Francis Wisconsin, published in Salesianum 10 (1914).

News, a major city paper, regularly defended Catholicism against slights both real and imagined.[32]

The 1860s were as peaceful in Milwaukee as they were in Chicago. The carping of the freethinkers died out as their audience became smaller and the German Catholic community became larger. By the end of the decade, the freethinkers were no longer a viable force in Milwaukee politics.[33]

But the tolerance of the 1860s gave way to tension in the 1870s. The newly established English-language diocesan newspaper, The Catholic Vindicator, began a campaign to convince Irish Catholics of the benefits of parochial education. As part of this effort, the Vindicator attacked the Protestant bias of the public schools. The persistent criticism perpetuated tension over education in Milwaukee.[34]

In 1874, the newly established German Catholic weekly, Die Columbia, joined the campaign. In March, the editors argued that the state had no right to interfere with the rights of individual citizens because the state drew its power from those very citizens. The state itself was no more than a collection of individually owned pieces of land and the rights of those landowners

32. Milwaukee Daily News, April 15, 1857.

33. Milwaukee Sentinel, April 26, 1861, July 25, 1863; Wisconsin Journal of Education, 6 (September 1861):80; (July 1861):14; (August 1861):44; 7 (October 1862):100; Annual Report of the Board of School Commissioners for the Year 1861 (Milwaukee, 1861); Annual Report . . . 1864, (Milwaukee, 1864); Annual Report . . . 1866, (Milwaukee, 1866).

34. Milwaukee Sentinel, March 15, 1873, April 29, December 24, 1874, July 25, 1875; The Catholic Vindicator, March 26, April 25, May 16, June 20, 1874.

should not be violated.[35]   In later issues, the editors complained about the "treacherous work of destruction" done in the
public schools and emphasized the duty of parents to provide a
good religious education for their children.[36]

Perhaps the most realistic assessment of the Catholic attack
on the injustices and failures of public education came in the
inaugural volume of the short-lived Milwaukee Catholic Magazine.
A September 1875 article entitled "Catholic Parents and the
School Dilemma" focused on the ineffectiveness of the Catholic
campaign for school funds. The anonymous author believed that no
amount of argument or rhetorical flourish by Catholic editors
would change the mind of the non-Catholic community. "Whatever
unfairness to Catholics there is," the author wrote, "or whatever
evils flow from these public schools is not our affair
. . . . The common schools do not hinder us from being
Christians; and we deceive ourselves when we think that a share
of the school fund would make us and better Catholics than we are
now . . . . Catholics are able to instruct their own children
without a share of the public money."[37] It was hardly the message that Catholic school advocates wanted to hear. Not surprisingly, the Milwaukee Catholic Magazine folded after a single year
of publication.

Throughout the 1870s, Milwaukee Catholics fought a number of
losing skirmishes over the content of public and parochial educa-

---

35. Die Columbia, March 12, 1874.

36. Ibid., February 4, 11, September 9, 23, October 28, 1875.

37. Milwaukee Catholic Magazine, 1 (September 1875).

tion. For the most part, Catholics sided with Democrats. In the election of 1875, for example, the Republicans accused the Democrats of scheming with Catholics to undermine the public schools.[38] Three years later, Catholic Democrats challenged the use of the King James Bible in state institutions.[39] Even though they lost all of their campaigns, Catholics learned from their involvement in the political arena. Most importantly, they learned that the Republicans were deaf to any Catholic appeals. This fact made the bond between Catholics and the Democratic Party even stronger.

The 1880s brought renewed Catholic criticism of public education. Both the Catholic Citizen, which replaced the Vindicator, and Die Columbia sustained the rhetorical attack. In 1880, the Citizen printed an article on the increasing number of Protestants to be found in Catholic boarding schools, a trend that was attributed to the strict moral code of these institutions.[40] Die Columbia implied that the exodus of Protestant students from the public schools was due to the mechanical nature of the instruction, the uncorrected immorality of the students, and

---

38. Sister M. Justile McDonald, The Irish in Wisconsin During the Nineteenth Century (Washington, 1954), pp. 159-163; Milwaukee Sentinel, December 11, 1875; December 8, 1876.

39. Milwaukee Sentinel, January 18, February 5, August 23, 1878.

40. Catholic Citizen, February 14, 1880, August 26, September 3, November 18, 1882.

the usurpation of the rights of the family by public school officials.[41]

A donnybrook over Catholic representation on the state boards of education also added to the tension. An editorial in the Citizen criticized the various boards of education for their lack of Catholic representation. The editors of the Milwaukee Sentinel disagreed. "We deny that Catholics or any other religious sect has a right to such representation," went the editorial. "The Boards in question should be selected without reference to sectarian opinions. Sectarianism is by law excluded from the educational system of the state."[42] The Citizen rebutted the Sentinel by noting that the population of the state was 25 percent Catholic and that a large minority deserved at least some representation o these boards.[43]

The Sentinel denied that there was any policy of excluding Catholics, but they wondered why a denomination so opposed to public education wanted to serve on these boards.[44] "Our right to a share in the control of public education," responded the Citizen, "is not contingent on our acceptance of its benefits. It grows out of our equal partnership in paying the expenses of the system."[45]

---

41. Die Columbia, November 15, 1880, September 8, 15, 22, 1881.

42. Milwaukee Sentinel, September 14, 16, 1883.

43. Catholic Citizen, September 22, 29, 1883.

44. Milwaukee Sentinel, September 24, 1883.

45. Catholic Citizen, October 13, 1883.

Like so many Catholic protests, nothing was done as a follow-up to this perceived injustice. Complaints in the Citizen and Die Columbia became a yearly ritual, reiterating the injustices of the school tax and the immorality of public schooling. In July 1884, the Citizen claimed yet again that the public school was the foe of Catholicism. Moreover, the paper noted that school officials took great pride and delight in knowing that Catholic children who attended public schools lost their faith. "The instinct of self preservation is called into play while the bigots are planning . . . to uproot Catholicity," added the editors, "it is not strange if the Bishops should assemble and arrive at a counter plan."[46]

With a lull in the agitation against public education, public school officials in Milwaukee began to push more forcefully for Americanization. "Our children must first and foremost be taught to read, write and speak English with facility and correctness," wrote the president of the school board in 1888. "They must be imbued with patriotic devotion to their country and its institutions and gain a liberal knowledge of American history, the fundamental laws and natural products and industries of our country. Although we may yield to the local interest of the community in regard to the instruction in a special foreign language, we must not forget that the schools are, first of all, American schools; and that whatever branch we introduce must be

---

46. Ibid., July 5, September 6, 1884; Die Columbia, December 11, 12, 1884.

taught with a view to making better citizens."[47] The superintendent reiterated this point when he emphasized American values for
the public school -- industry, frugality, patience and obedience
to proper authority.

Public school advocates kept up a steady drumbeat of concern
throughout the 1880s. They repeatedly asked the state to take
action against ethnically oriented religious parochial schools.
A new Republican governor, William Hoard, sponsored a number of
reforms in the state's child welfare and compulsory education
laws. Even though previous legislation required the attendance
of all children at school and instruction in English, these laws
had not been enforced. Hoard hoped to reinforce these laws with
more rigorous legislation.

State Senator Levi Pond introduced the first such bill in
1889. The legislation would require annual statistical reports
from private as well as public schools to enable the state to
judge whether sufficient English instruction was being provided.
When news of the bill leaked out, the protest was overwhelming.
The tremendous German American resistance to the very idea of
regulation killed the bill in the state Senate.

At the same time, however, the lower house passed a similar
piece of legislation sponsored by Michael Bennett, a young Irish
Catholic legislator from Pine Knot. The Bennett bill was a copy
of the Edwards Law which had passed the Illinois legislature
without opposition. Bennett's bill required compulsory atten-

47. Annual Report of the Board of the Board of School
Commissioners for the Year 1888 (Milwaukee, 1888), p. 23.

dance of all children in some public or private school, but only those institutions using English as the principal language would be considered schools. The eventual passage of the Bennett bill in the Senate and its later passage into law triggered a major upheaval in the balance of power in the state.[48]

The law primarily affected German Lutheran and German Catholic schools and the protests from these groups was immediate and persistent. The Wisconsin Synod of the Lutheran Church, meeting in June 1889, declared the law "tyrannical and unjust" because it "jeopardizes the permanency of our loyal parochial schools [and] . . . permits unjustified encroachment upon parental rights and family life."[49] Both Die Columbia and Germania, the German Lutheran weekly, soundly rejected the law and persisted in their criticism of it throughout the summer and fall of 1889. Even a letter from Bennett himself, published in the Sentinel in October, did not convince the Germans that the law was not part of an underhanded plot against their heritage.[50]

The controversy escalated during the first six months of 1890. In December 1889, the German Lutherans had formed a state-wide committee to organize opposition to the law.[51] In March, the Catholic bishops in Wisconsin issued a formal state-

---

48. Jensen, Winning of the Midwest, pp. 123-153; Paul Kleppner, The Cross of Culture (Glencoe, 1971); McDonald, Irish in Wisconsin.

49. Lutheran Witness, July 21, 1889, as cited in Jensen, Winning of the Midwest, p. 124.

50. Milwaukee Sentinel, October 2, 1889.

51. Ibid., December 30, 1889; Jensen, Winning of the Midwest, p. 126.

ment on the law. Noting that the law interfered with the rights of the Church and the parent, the bishops saw the law as "the further object of entirely eliminating the parochial schools.[52] In April, the Democrats captured a majority of the votes in the Milwaukee municipal elections by emphasizing their opposition to the Bennett Law. In June, the anti-Bennett Law forces met in convention to compare strategies. Out of this convention came a series of Anti-Bennett Law Clubs to solicit votes for their cause. The Catholics and the Lutherans were meeting for the first time under the banner of the Democratic party and this deeply worried Republican professionals in the state.[53]

Unfortunately for the Republicans, their standard bearer was a poor politician -- George Hoard, the incumbent governor and dairy farming pioneer. Even though his staff advised changes in the law, Hoard thought the law a good one and he decided to make it an issue in the campaign. The governor claimed that he had received tens of thousands of letters from German farmers supporting his position; he felt sure of victory.

The Democrats quickly took the opposite position at their state convention in August. They denounced the law as "unwise, unconstitutional, unAmerican, and undemocratic."[54] Hoard's rhetoric became frantic as the campaign wore on. His friends plastered the state with signs saying "The Little Red

---

52. _Milwaukee Journal_, March 12, 1890; Jensen, _Winning of the Midwest_, p. 126.

53. _Ibid._, p. 127; Kleppner, _Cross of Culture_, pp. 164-165.

54. _Chicago Tribune_, August 27, 28, 1890; Jensen, _Winning of the Midwest_, p. 133.

Schoolhouse: STAND BY IT!" but it was a futile gesture. The Democrats swept Hoard and other major Republicans from office. It was a devastating defeat made worse by the aggravated rhetoric of George Hoard.

The Catholic Citizen took steps to make sure that the election was not misinterpreted. "We do not attack the public school system," wrote the editors a month before the election. "Our contemporary [the Sentinel] cannot quote a single expression from this journal attacking the public school system. We are willing to criticize although we have not done even that [in the election campaign] to our knowledge. Neither does the opposition to the Bennett Law, Lutheran, Democratic, or Catholic attack the public schools . . . . The only people who are putting the public schools in controversy are the Bennett Law people."[55]

The Citizen emphasized that the Church wanted no more than to preserve the status quo against the encroachment of Republicans. "The Citizen believes that the masses of the Republican party in Wisconsin are liberal men who intended no harm to Church schools, and preferred no interference with them. But the Bennett Law drew all the sectarian, bigoted, fanatical, and crazy impurities in the Republican party to a head and the consequent boil governed the Republican party rather than its brains."[56]

Both contemporary observers and present day historians tend to agree with the Citizen's estimate of the problem. "The defeat was inevitable," wrote Senator John Spooner to an associate.

55. Catholic Citizen, October 4, 1890.

56. Ibid., November 8, 1890.

"The school law did it -- a silly, sentimental and damned useless abstraction, foisted upon us by a self righteous demagogue."[57] Spooner's anger with Hoard was understandable. The loss of the Republican majority in the state legislature meant that Spooner was not to be re-elected to the Senate.

Yet other dispassionate assessments also blame Hoard. "The anti-Bennett campaign was not a crusade, but a counter crusade," notes Richard Jensen. "Hoard was the crusader -- the amateur politician rallying the people in their righteousness to prevent the corruption of public education and smite the evil of priestly control of Wisconsin politics."[58] The entire affair might never have taken place had Hoard listened to Spooner and other Republican professionals.

All of this is not to minimize the importance of the victory won by the Catholic-Lutheran coalition. Catholics learned not only that minorities could win at the polls, but also the importance of building coalitions in winning such victories. Had the Catholics stood alone against Hoard and the Bennett Law, they would have lost the election. But in with joining the Lutherans, the Church found political strength. Such coalitions were only temporary, and the two denominations did not agree on more than opposition to the Bennett Law, but where the occasion arose, such means were possible. Catholic leaders, henceforth looked for ways to appeal to other religious groups with common grievances.

---

57. Spooner to H.M. Kulitin, November 18, 1890, Spooner Papers, Library of Congress, as cited in Jensen, Winning of the Midwest, p. 122.

58. Jensen, Winning of the Midwest, p. 147.

The defeat of the Republicans and the Bennett Law in 1890 marked the end of a long period of struggle for the Catholic Church. By 1890, they understood how the system worked and had tasted victory.

IV

The defeat of the Bennett Law had the same ramifications as the defeat of the Edwards Law; together these Catholic victories constituted a turning point in church-state relations in education. They were two conflicts among many which clarified the prerogatives of the state in regard to private schools. In addition, the repeal of the two laws marked a pause in the educational debate in Chicago and Milwaukee and secured the independence of Catholic parochial schools in both cities.

In Milwaukee as in Chicago, public and Catholic school advocates argued over the justice of common schooling for forty years with no apparent affect on either side. Yet real changes had taken place. The public schools of Milwaukee and Chicago, under pressure from the Catholic community and other concerned groups, abandoned Biblical instruction and adopted a curriculum that separated religion from education. The parochial schools, under pressure from public schoolmen became increasingly American in form and content.

The disagreements over schooling in those cities persisted throughout the nineteenth century and well into the twentieth precisely because both public and parochial school advocates shared a common belief in the importance of education. "If on any one point, the friends and enemies of the Catholic Church are a unit," wrote Josef Salzmann, "it is on the question of the importance of the schools. Both hold the view that the future belongs to him that controls the schools."[59]

59. Quoted in Harry Heming, ed., <u>The Catholic Church in Wisconsin</u>, (4 vols., Milwaukee, 1895-1899), 1:172

CHAPTER III

THE DYNAMICS OF CATHOLIC DIOCESAN LEADERSHIP

I

"I am the good shepherd," Christ proclaims in John 10: 14-16, "I know my own and my own know me, just as the Father knows me and I know the Father; and I lay down my life for my sheep. And there are other sheep I have that are not of this fold and these I have to lead as well. They too will listen to my voice, and there will be only one flock and one shepherd." Certainly the "good shepherd" was the role model that the Catholic Church intended for her bishops. And in many nations around the world, Catholic bishops were good shepherds of placid, homogeneous flocks.

But the American Catholic Church in the nineteenth century faced a set of circumstances that challenged even the best bishops. Disobedient priests, rebellious laymen, inter-ethnic rivalries, and other factors made it difficult for the men selected by Rome to lead their flocks in American dioceses. More than one American priest turned away from the Holy Father's call, dreading the problems of diocesan leadership. More than one bishop was institutionalized or retired prematurely unable to cope with the tensions of the American Catholic prelacy.

Yet it is difficult to make generalizations about the dynamics of Catholic diocesan leadership. To be sure, every American

bishop faced difficult challenges, but each bishop responded dif-
ferently.   Each prelate brought different strengths and weak-
nesses to the position and the number and severity of the problems faced by each man were also different.   One need only compare the challenges faced by John Hughes of New York with those
of Jean Lamy of Santa Fe to appreciate these differences.[1]   If
There is any constant in the various experiences of American
Catholic bishops, it is that successful bishops led their flocks
by using a variety of interpersonal skills, not by using the
authority of canon law.

II

When William Quarter arrived in Chicago to take control of
his new diocese, he faced a number of administrative problems not
the least of which was a growing trustee movement.   Lay trustees
held title to Church property in the new diocese and were reluctant to surrender their power.   But the new bishop had previous
experience with trustees in New York and he was confident he
could solve the problem.   He petitioned the Illinois General
Assembly to settle the question of land ownership.   "This bill,
if it passes," Quarter wrote in January 1845, "will obviate the
necessity of anything in the form of trusteeism in this diocese
forever.   There is not a trustee in this diocese, nor shall there

---

1. For contrasting portraits of these men and their leadership
styles, see Jay P. Dolan, The Immigrant Church: New York's Irish
and German Catholics (Baltimore, 1975); Richard Shaw, Dagger
John: The Life and Times of Archbishop John Hughes (New York,
1977); and Paul Horgan, Lamy of Santa Fe: His Life and Times (New
York, 1975).

be as long as I live."[2]   The passage of the bill in February
pleased Quarter very much.   "The bill was well-supported by the
Protestant members of this city . . . . This settles the independence of bishops and priests here forever -- no trustees
now!"[3]

Two other issues emerged during Quarter's tenure which
caused trouble not only for him but also for his successors.
With the settlement of substantial numbers of German and French
Catholics in Chicago during the late 1840s, ethnic hostility between these groups and the Irish became a major concern.   How
would the Germans and the French relate to an Irish bishop, and
where would that Irish bishop find German and French priests to
staff ethnic parishes?[4]   Even though he was able to establish two
German parishes, Quarter was unable to find enough German priests
to meet the demand.   His sudden death in 1848 left the problem
unsolved.

A second problem was Quarter's control over the priests and
religious in his diocese.   The insatiable need for priests and
nuns in his parishes forced Quarter to accept almost every religious who came his way, and together they formed a motley collection with divergent loyalties.   Some were renegades from other
dioceses, others were missionaries with allegiances only to their
religious orders.   Quarter had no significant authority over many

---

2. Quarter to Bishop Blanc of New Orleans, January 17, 1845,
copy in the AAC.

3. Quarter to Hughes, February 28, 1845, AAC.

4. Quarter to the Leopoldine Association, Vienna, December 20,
1845, AAC.

of his priests except for canon law and Catholic tradition, but these counted for little on the frontier.

Premature death released Quarter from the burdens of diocesan leadership in 1848, but the problems remained for his successor. Even though James Van de Velde was an intelligent and capable leader, he did not have the skills needed to unite Quarter's loose confederation of parishes. Under Quarter, each parish remained financially and administratively independent and efforts by Van de Velde to assert his authority led to his downfall.[5]

The feisty independence of the German parishes, in concert with a rebellion among the professors at the University of St. Mary of the Lake, dramatized the fragile nature of diocesan authority and leadership in Chicago. Exercising the canonical prerogatives of his office early in 1852, Van de Velde assigned an Irish pastor to the heavily German St. Peter's parish. The parishioners vigorously protested what they believed to be an abridgment of their right to a German pastor. "They seemed determined to stop at nothing," wrote Van de Velde, "however criminal or sacrilegious their proceedings . . . they have had recourse to all sorts of lawlessness and violent means to force the bishop of this diocese to remove the pastor from the congregation over which he has placed him, or to drive him off by repeated

---

5. Diary of James O. Van de Velde, as reprinted in James J. McGovern, _Souvenir of the Silver Jubilee in the Episcopacy of Patrick A. Feehan_ (Chicago, 1891), pp. 11-115, 144, 162.

arrogances."[6] Trouble also emerged in St. Michael's parish where even a German pastor did not mollify the Congregation. Van de Velde had a full-sized rebellion among his German parishioners by mid-1852.

St. Peter's and St. Michael's reflected the two principal facets of Van de Velde's problem with diocesan leadership. The overwhelming religious concern of the Germans was to find pastors who would respond to the needs of the parish community. All acceptable candidates necessarily had to be German-born to understand the culture. Moreover, these candidates had to pledge their loyalty to the parish which supported them. At St. Peter's the appointment of an Irishman violated the first criteria; no Irish pastor could understand the German mentality. At St. Michael's the pastor pledged his loyalty to the bishop rather than his parish and the Germans rebelled. In effect, both German parishes rejected the authority of the bishop to decide unilaterally on parish appointments. Since pastors ministered to clearly defined communities, the Germans thought those communities should have a voice in the decision-making process.

The last vestiges of Van de Velde's authority collapsed with the revolt of the university faculty in March and April 1852. The professors involved themselves in the dispute between Van de Velde and the Germans, offering moral support and encouragement to the latter. When Van de Velde dismissed them, they refused to leave, claiming obedience only to the superiors of their reli-

---

6. Western Tablet, March 20, 1852; Souvenir of the Golden Jubilee of St. Peter's Friary, 1875-1925 (Chicago, 1925), p. 12.

gious orders. "They have used their endeavors," wrote Van de Velde to his colleagues, "to form a party averse to the Bishop among the clergy and have in some measure succeeded. The leader of the party is the head of the University of St. Mary of the Lake and has taken such measures that the bishop is forced to keep him in office for fear of having a suit instituted against him and of perhaps seeing the Catholics of Chicago involved in schism or acting in opposition to his authority."[7] While he stayed in Chicago for another year, Van de Velde was only a titular leader of the diocese; his university and his parishes were virtually autonomous.

These independent parishes confronted Van de Velde's successor, Anthony O'Regan, when he arrived in Chicago in 1854. In appealing to John Henni of Milwaukee for German and French priests, O'Regan noted the hostility that greeted him upon his arrival in the diocese. "There are serious difficulties in this diocese," he wrote, "I dread to encounter them. Differences here are altogether unlike what I have known elsewhere."[8] The bishop's inability to find foreign priests to serve in his German and French parishes made conflicts inevitable. The Germans in St. Michael's parish were so rebellious that they had a new pastor nearly every

---

7. Van de Velde to the Congregation of the Most Reverence Archbishops, May 1, 1852, AAC; "Diary of James O. Van de Velde," October 27, 1853, in Souvenir of the Episcopacy of Patrick Feehan, p. 184. It is interesting to note that neither of the reasons for his resignation -- poor health or inability to govern -- were recorded in his diary. See Souvenir of Patrick Feehan, pp. 186-196.

8. O'Regan to Henni, November 6, 1854; O'Regan to Richard Purcell, January 26, 1855; O'Regan to Peter R. Kenrick, May 19, 1855, copies in AAC.

other year during the 1850s. The French Catholics in St. Louis'
parish carried their objections to the public when an Irish
priest replaced a rebellious Frenchman as pastor. Petitions published in the Chicago Tribune claimed that O'Regan violated his
promise to appoint a French pastor, and the lay leaders of the
parish condemned the bishop as a tyrant.[9] Both parishes demanded
priests of their own nationality as if such appointments were a
right rather than a privilege.[10]

Unable to handle the constant tension, O'Regan resigned his
appointment in May 1858 and chose to retire at the rather young
age of forty-five. His limitations as a leader, according to his
critics, were due to his unwillingness to compromise his episcopal prerogatives. This feeling was expressed best in a letter to
the Tribune regarding O'Regan's successor: "We will expect a man
of more practical and social knowledge," wrote one Chicago Catholic. "It may not be out of place to suggest that one of the old
clergymen of the diocese might practically be the best . . . who
will know the wants of the people. Experience has partially
demonstrated, particularly in the case of Bishop O'Regan, that a
stranger from another diocese will scarcely comprehend the proper
method of establishing his episcopal influence in a diocese cir-
cumstanced as ours has been for some time."[11]

---

9. Chicago Tribune, January 26, March 13, 1857.

10. Ibid., August 25, September 16, November 3, 1857; May 20,
1858.

11. Chicago Tribune, May 20, 1858.

Perhaps Rome was listening to the Catholics of Chicago because the new bishop was familiar with the diocese. James Duggan had served as the administrator of the diocese in 1854 between the tenures of Van de Velde and O'Regan. He was a popular man in St. Louis and liked well enough in Chicago during his brief stay. The American bishops thought him to be a good choice, and the early years of Duggan's administration seemed to prove the bishops correct.[12]

The Van de Velde and O'Regan years had been consumed by inter-ethnic bitterness, but Duggan avoided the problem by obtaining commitments of priests from a number of German religious orders. The Franciscans took charge of three parishes and the Benedictines and Redemptorists took one each.[13] In addition, Duggan reestablished the University of St. Mary of the Lake, another O'Regan problem, and put the John McMullen, a Chicago-born, Vatican-trained priest, in charge. On the surface, the administration of Chicago seemed different under Duggan than it had been under his predecessors.

But tension began to mount in 1866 when petty squabbling broke off the previously amicable relation between Duggan and

---

12. For Duggan's background, see George S. Phillips, Chicago and her Churches (Chicago, 1868). James P. Gaffey, "Patterns of Ecclesiastical Authority: The Problem of Chicago's Succession, 1865-1881," Church History 42 (June 1973): 257-271; Souvenir of Patrick Feehan, pp. 196-201.

13. Bessie L. Pierce, A History of Chicago (3 vols., New York, 1937-57), 2:360-363; The New World, Centennial Edition, April 14, 1900; Gilbert Garraghan, The History of the Catholic Church in Chicago, 1643-1871 (Chicago, 1922), pp. 194-195, 205-206; Joseph J. Thompson, The Archdiocese of Chicago (Chicago, 1920), pp. 33-40.

some of his most powerful priests. Some unrevealed trouble between Duggan and McMullen caused the bishop to close the seminary and the university. Fights between Duggan and Dennis Dunne, who served as vicar general as well as parish pastor, led to Dunne's dismissal from his diocesan post. Both McMullen and Dunne were well-respected members of the Catholic community and their dismissals caused great consternation among the priests and laity alike.

In the midst of this crisis, Duggan was told that a long rest away from Chicago was necessary if he was to recover from a lingering illness. Before leaving, however, he divided his authority between two young and inexperienced priests: one to be in charge of the German parishes, and the other to be in charge of finances. This action climaxed the struggle between Duggan and his diocese. McMullen, Dunne, the rector of the seminary, and the rector of the cathedral petitioned the Vatican to reassign Duggan to another diocese.[14]

Duggan was outraged when he heard about the petition; he returned to Chicago and suspended the four priests. Even though a Church investigation into the matter cleared Duggan of any canonical impropriety, the laity of the diocese remained upset. McMullen traveled to Rome to make a personal appeal for the removal of the bishop, and the secular press gave play to the issue

---

14. Gaffey, "Pattern," pp. 258-262; Daniel Riordan, "University of St. Mary of the Lake," Illinois Catholic Historical Review 2 (October 1919): 135-160; "Report of the Archbishop Peter R. Kenrick to Cardinal Barnabo of the Congregation of Religious Doctrine," August 10, 1868, copy in AAC.

in Chicago.[15] Unable to handle the rebellion, Duggan became des-
pondent and attempted suicide on two occasions. Late in 1868, he
was committed to the Asylum of the Sisters of Charity in St.
Louis.

Because Duggan did not resign and Rome was unwilling to remove him from his post, a diocesan administrator was appointed as
a replacement. Bishop Thomas Foley arrived in Chicago as the
auxiliary bishop of the diocese; his task of uniting the parishes
into some form of central administration was difficult at best.
Foley decided that a low profile would be best; during the ten
years of his administration in Chicago, he never gave an inter-
view to the press, never voted in a municipal election nor involved himself in public affairs. He reappointed John McMullen
to a position of responsibility and generally sought to make
peace with the corps of pastors in the diocese. Moreover, Foley
organized the search for aid and assistance in the reconstruction
of over one million dollars worth of churches and schools lost in
the fire of October 1871. Foley did his best to heal old wounds
and to allay fears that he was a power-mad prelate.[16]

This is not to say that Foley did not make progress in the
assertion of diocesan authority and leadership. It was during
Foley's tenure that a Catholic bishop in Chicago effectively disciplined his subordinates for the first time. Foley dismissed a

---

15. Chicago Tribune, August 14, September 21, 27, October 1,
7, 12, 13, 16, 1868; Chicago Times, September 21, 27, 28, 30,
October 12, 18, 1868; Dunne to John Henni, September 25, 1868,
McMullen to Henni, September 26, 1868, ASFS.

16. For a sketch of Foley, see Souvenir of Patrick Feehan,
pp. 202-226.

priest named John M. Ryan for bad conduct and debauchery; Ryan sued the bishop in Circuit Court, but Foley was upheld.[17]   He disciplined a second priest, Edward A. Terry, for his unorthodox views on the interpretation of the Bible.[18]   Foley also was able to rid the diocese of a splinter group of the Sisters of Loretto. Even though the _Tribune_ played up the "cruelty of the affair," Foley's reputation for fairness remained intact.[19]

A final challenge to Foley's episcopal authority came from a renegade priest and the lay trustees of Holy Trinity Church, a Polish parish. Because the trustees refused to deed the property to the diocese, Foley did not assign a priest to the parish. The appearance of one "Father Melcuzney" added to the problem and Foley closed the church until Melcuzney abandoned his masquerade. The trustees attempted a compromise: the property would be surrendered in exchange for the approval of Melcuzney. But Foley would have nothing to do with the parish and eventually forced the rebels to surrender.[20] By 1878, Foley had made substantial progress in establishing the powers and prerogatives of the episcopacy in Chicago.

Foley's achievements as an administrator are difficult to explain. Part of his success can be attributed to his low profile and his appeals for diocesan harmony. Indeed, Chicago was

---

17. _Chicago Times_, August 22, 1873.

18. Pierce, _History of Chicago_, 3:433; _Chicago Times_, June 4, 6, 1874.

19. _Chicago Tribune_, August 20, 1874.

20. _Chicago Tribune_, April 17, 22, 1877.

ready for peace by 1870. After twenty years of diocesan bicker-
ing and unrest, little had been gained by either side. Chicago
Catholics were tired and Foley offered no visible threats to
their self-defined religious liberties. If he demanded loyalty
from his parishes, he also granted them substantial autonomy.
Another encouragement for ecclesiastical peace resulted from the
devastation of Chicago by fire. If the city and the diocese were
to rebuild, substantial cooperation was necessary. Foley's administration broke with the past and a new era of cooperation
existed in Chicago.

Foley's sudden death in February 1879 caused the press to
speculate on the leadership needs of the diocese. "A man of rare
combination of admirable qualities is needed," wrote the editors
of the Chicago Times, " the man must have great executive abilities and be endowed with perfect tact. The place needs a man of
unusual lofty stature in administrative talent and one who could
gracefully adorn the exaltation of conspicuous rank."[21] The editors of the Tribune believed that the selection of Patrick A.
Feehan, the Bishop of Nashville was an excellent choice.[22]
Indeed, the administration of Patrick Augustus Feehan, first
Archbishop of Chicago, was largely without turmoil and marked the
beginning of a coordinated administration for the diocese.

Feehan succeeded because he followed Foley's example. "The
secret of his success," notes historian Charles Shanabruch, "was

---

21. Chicago Times, April 21, 1879; Chicago Tribune, April 13,
1879.

22. Chicago Tribune, September 1, 1880.

real respect for the judgment of his priests. By permitting them
wide latitude in their parishes, he gave them a sense of independence and importance, and in return received their support for
his diocesan programs."[23]   Feehan regularly visited his parishes
to demonstrate his concern for the welfare and interests of the
laity.

He accepted the existing network of territorial and national
parishes and worked with religious orders to staff many parishes.
"Although the jurisdictional, personnel, and financial problems
attendant to the tripling of the number of parishes was great, he
held the system together by his flexibility, and adaptability.
He placed loyal and capable men in the chancery, selected a
'balanced ticket' for his advisory council, shared his authority
with religious-order superiors, and encouraged initiative on the
local level."[24]   After decades of turmoil, Catholic Chicago was
finally at peace with its "shepherd."

III

When John Martin Henni arrived in Milwaukee to take over his
new appointment, he began a tenure of over thirty years. His accomplishments included two orphanages, a normal school, a seminary, two school societies, and sixteen parochial schools, all
built between 1844 and 1878.[25]   The reasons for Henni's success

---

23. Charles Shanabruch, Chicago's Catholics: The Evolution of
an American Identity (Notre Dame, 1981), p. 37.

24. Ibid., p. 53.

25. Frank Flower, History of Milwaukee (Chicago, 1881),
pp. 891-193.   Anthony Fischer, "History of the St. Amelian's

were partly due to chance and partly the result of strong, well-experienced leadership.

Yet Henni's tenure was not without turmoil. The problems of inter-ethnic hostility -- so much a part of Chicago -- were also present in Milwaukee. Henni utilized the ethnic parish as a means of preventing conflict, but even at his retirement, inter-ethnic hostility was a potent, disruptive force in the diocese. The history of the Henni administration portrays the subtle dynamics of diocesan leadership.

Before becoming the first bishop of Milwaukee, Henni had been a priest in Cincinnati. He had established the first German Catholic newspaper in the United States and he achieved notoriety for his skills in settling trustee problems between the Irish bishop and his German parishes. Above all, Henni had many friends -- priests who later came to his aid in Milwaukee. In fact, Martin Kundig, Michael Heiss, and Josef Salzmann became the nucleus of Henni's administration. Kundig, an experienced missionary in Michigan and Wisconsin and Henni's vicar general, was a friend from seminary days. Heiss, the first rector of the diocesan seminary in Milwaukee and Henni's successor as Archbishop, was a friend from Cincinnati. Salzmann, Henni's chief fund raiser, was another Cincinnati friend. All three priests were German, capable in their leadership, and devoted to Henni. Their

Orphan Asylum, 1849-1928" (unpub. M.A. thesis, St. Francis Seminary, 1928), p. 7.

teamwork on many projects under Henni's guidance accounted for much of the institutional growth in the diocese.[26]

Yet eventual progress was not evident upon Henni's arrival. Like its sister diocese to the south, Milwaukee suffered from a trustee problem. Experience had prepared Henni and his priests for this trouble. In Cincinnati, Henni had undercut a trustee rebellion in one parish by calling a general meeting of loyal parishioners to condemn the rebels. The weight of public opinion buckled the revolt. In Detroit in 1843, Kundig dissipated a trustee problem by calling a parish meeting to discuss the issue of property ownership. After discussion, a vote was taken which supported the bishop. What the trustees did not know was that Kundig had packed the meeting with outsiders. Henni and Kundig applied this experience to two parishes, one in Burlington, Wisconsin, and the other in New Bristol, Wisconsin, and their skills prevented these problems from growing into major incidents.[27]

With trustee problems on the decline, Henni turned his attention to more pressing issues in his new diocese. Like Quarter, Henni focused on two issues that were critical to the growth of the new diocese: finding competent teachers to establish Catholic schools and finding the funds to support these

---

26. For information on the lives of these three leaders and their relationship to one another, see Peter L. Johnson, Stuffed Saddlebags (Milwaukee, 1942); Peter L. Johnson, The Crosier on the Frontier (Madison, 1959); Joseph Ranier, A Noble Priest (Milwaukee, 1903); M. Mileta Ludwig, Right Hand Glove Uplifted (New York, 1968).

27. Alfred Strich, "Trusteeism in the Old Northwest, 1880-1850," Catholic Historical Review 30 (July 1944): 160-163. Johnson, Stuffed Saddlebags, pp. 77-80.

schools. In both areas Henni surpassed the achievements of his
colleagues in Chicago. In 1846, Henni obtained a contingent of
the Sisters of Charity to establish a hospital, an orphanage, and
to teach the English-speaking children.[28] The needs of the Irish
parishioners were not great, and the Sisters were able to meet
expectations.

But Henni faced an immense problem in providing teachers for
the mushrooming German Catholic schools. He needed German
teaching sisters in great numbers, and any news of the arrival of
such an order gave him great hope. "To my joy," he wrote in
1846, "I was told in Baltimore that the School Sisters of Bavaria
are expected. I hope I may get some of them for the benefit of
our young German people. There is not a doubt that not a few
would join them from the west and thus enlarge their community."[29]

Henni's wish was not fulfilled quickly, and he became anxious. "How is it that you have nothing to say whether the
School Sisters really intend to come to Milwaukee," he wrote to
his friend Joseph Mueller in Bavaria. "I am anxious to know
whether this, my wish, could be fulfilled before the year is
over."[30] The School Sisters of Notre Dame finally arrived in

---

28. Henni to Mother Xavier of the Sisters of Charity,
Emmitsburg, Md., January 1, 1845, cited in Daniel O'Hearn, Fifty
Years at St. John's Cathedral, 1847-1897 (Milwaukee, n.d.),
p. 34.

29. Henni to Mueller, August 7, 1846, ASFS, printed in
Salesianum 37 (1942).

30. Henni to Mueller, January 24, 1848, ASFS, printed in
Salesianum 38 (1943).

Milwaukee in 1851 after Henni raised the money for their support. It was an investment well worth the time and effort since Milwaukee became the North American headquarters for this order.

The second problem facing Henni was funding. In this regard Henni's friendship with Joseph Mueller was invaluable. Mueller was the chaplain of the Ludwig Mission Society, a German charity that distributed substantial amounts of money to the American missions.[31] Mueller's advocacy of the Wisconsin diocese undoubtedly obtained larger sums than Henni might have received without the chaplain's help. Moreover, "no bishop was better known by the missionary aid societies in Europe than was Henni. These societies contributed sizeable sums to the diocese in its first three critical years, and did not falter in their financial assistance throughout its initial quarter century."[32] Henni was most fortunate in obtaining funds not only from the Ludwig Mission Society but also the Association for the Propagation of the Faith in France and the Leopoldine Society in Austria.

Henni used these funds to help build a motherhouse for the School Sisters of Notre Dame. He took a personal interest in the design and construction and later remembered it as one of his greatest achievements. Yet it was the decision of Mother Caroline Freiss to move her order from Baltimore to Milwaukee

---

31. Mueller to Henni, May 20, 1847, printed in Theodore Roemer, The Ludwigmissionsverein and the Church in the United States, 1838-1918 (Washington, 1933), pp. 35-36; Henni to Mueller, March 27, 1848, printed in Salesianum 38 (1943).

32. Peter L. Johnson, "Antecedents of St. Francis Seminary in Milwaukee," Wisconsin Magazine of History 40 (Autumn 1956), p. 41.

which relieved Henni of his German teacher problems. The new motherhouse was able to meet the majority of Henni's needs. "The motherhouse is of particular credit for Milwaukee," Michael Heiss wrote in 1861, "it is in a flourishing condition and sends its teachers to Catholic parishes throughout Wisconsin."[33] The dominance of the school sisters gave a certain homogeneity to the parochial schools which gave Catholic education in Milwaukee a sense of order unknown in Chicago.

Yet, it was an order that reflected ethnic group isolation rather than cooperation. "The main area of German settlement was sufficiently large in size, sufficiently diverse in living environment, varying from crowded central shop cum residence quarters to neat suburban rows, from gardened villas to squatter shanties to be a genuine microcosm of a complete city."[34]

Irish identity developed not so much out of ethnicity as it did out of politics, the temperance movement, and the Church. The Irish, however, had a difficult time in the face of overwhelming German dominance. "The Irish were unable to support their own newspaper or political association and evidenced some difficulty in maintaining fire companies . . . . Irish identity was evidently defined in terms of the interests of the laboring classes and lacked the diversity of the German image."[35]

---

33. Heiss to Ludwigmissionsverein, August 30, 1861, printed in Salesianum 40 (1945).

34. Kathleen N. Conzen, "The German Athens: Milwaukee and the Accommodation of Its Immigrants, 1836-1860." (unpub. Ph.D. dissertation, University of Wisconsin–Madison, 1972), pp. 9-13.

35. Ibid.

Henni was able to earn the respect of both the Germans and the Irish by organizing his diocese around the ethnic parish. Each ethnic group received its share of funds from the diocese and priests were assigned to parishes on the basis of national origin. Such a policy pleased not only the laity but also the priests. Yet such a policy also had its drawbacks as the Church in Milwaukee became a collection of ethno-centric islands; the Irish and the Germans communicated with Henni but not with each other.

This isolation produced a substantial amount of tension between the two groups. "Rivalry among the various nationalistic groups," wrote Heiss in the mid-1850s, "is frequently a real nuisance over here, and at the present, in a time of Know Nothingism, you may not even talk much against it without running the risk of being considered a secret Know Nothing."[36]

The dominance of the German community made Milwaukee a bilingual city and tension emerged between the German Catholic residents and the Irish Catholic residents. "Our neighborhood," remembered one resident, "gave ample proof of the clannishness which may beset a people of the same racial origin. They doted on the virtues of their own race and derided the vices of others. The Irish, who lived in a district south of our own, were regarded as being a shiftless people who contributed the largest quota to the House of Correction and the Poorhouse. The prejudice against them was usually enhanced when an Irishman called a

---

36. Heiss to Ludwigmissionsverein, January 21, 1855, copy in ASFS, printed in Salesianum 39 (1944): 118.

German-born a "damned Dutchman" or ridiculed his broken English. In retaliation for the slight, the other would be called an irischer Lump."[37]

There was no easy solution to the problem of inter-ethnic conflict. Some Catholics thought that enlightened teachers might educate the children to be more tolerant of one another. But the need for more teachers as well as an institution to train them prevented the immediate implementation of this plan.

The need for better schools remained self-evident. By the middle of 1868, Josef Salzmann argued that the "remedy for the evil of the age is the solid education of the young, but the years of schooling are all too short and the methods of teaching are frequently very poor, though we occasionally find a good teacher. We must found schools that are not merely drilling machines, but that are nurseries of faith, upbuilders of the whole man with all his facilities, the intellectual, the moral, the physical."[38]

Salzmann had high hopes for a normal school, seeing it as a place where the American and the Catholic educational ideal might complement each other to help the immigrant American teacher transcend the limitations of ethnicity. "I am comforted by the hope," he wrote to his friends, "that the disgusting features of nationality will be eliminated by the new institution because we intend to admit only German pupils and train them thoroughly in

---

37. William G. Bruce, "Memoirs," Wisconsin Magazine of History, 17 (1934): 10.

38. Ranier, A Noble Priest, pp. 172, 180.

the English language in order to have them participate as
teachers in the state schools through which school taxes also are
directed for the maintenance of teachers."[39]   Perhaps Michael
Heiss best summed up the spirit of the Catholic normal school
movement. "For the perfection of the Catholic school system," he
wrote, "this normal school is indispensable. Various careful con-
siderations have always led to the same conclusion."[40]

But the normal school was ineffective in breaking down the
barriers between ethic groups, and the arrival of Italians and
Poles in Milwaukee after 1870 created additional problems. Along
with the Irish these later groups chaffed at the German domina-
tion of the Church in Milwaukee, but no action was taken until
1878.[41] In the beginning of that year, Henni turned his attention to the search for a successor. As with many bishops who
look toward retirement, Henni asked the Vatican to name a "co-
adjutor" bishop who would eventually succeed him. The names
Henni submitted were all German and prospective appointment of
another German as bishop precipitated a major controversy within
the diocese.

39. Salzmann to Ludwigmissionsverein, April 20, 1872, copy in
ASFS, printed in Salesianum 42 (1947): 169-170; Die Columbia,
June 25, 1874.

40. Michael Heiss in the Pastoral Blatt 10 (June 1868): 114;
Valery Schuster, "The Catholic Normal School of the Holy Family
and Pio Nono College" (unpub. M.A. thesis, St. Francis Seminary,
1941), p. 2; Heiss to Kleiner, June 22, 1868, copy in ASFS,
printed in Salesianum 12 (1916).

41. Gerd Korman, Immigrants, Industrialists, and Americanizers: The View from Milwaukee, 1866-1920 (Madison, 1965), pp.
48-49.

Henni's action aroused the concern of the Irish priests of the diocese who wrote to James Cardinal Gibbons of Baltimore. Their principal concern was the "germanization" of the diocese. "These German priests have frequent meetings," wrote the Reverend George L. Willard, the editor of the Catholic Citizen, "the principal ulterior objective is to perpetuate a young Germany here . . . . Their endeavors are to make everything foreign and German and to make them obnoxious to Americans."[42] The priests believed that the German clerics were determined to keep all the power and authority of the diocese to themselves.[43]

Henni had not followed the guidelines for the appointment of a successor, and the Vatican informed the archbishop that he had to seek the advice of the bishops in his province.[44] On the evening before the meeting of the bishops, the Martin Kundig asked Bishop Thomas Grace of St. Paul to suggest the name of John Lancaster Spalding for the post of co-adjutor. Spalding was the bishop of Peoria, fluent both in English and in German, and very popular with the Catholics of Milwaukee. At the meeting, Grace's suggestion found little support and only after substantial discussion was Spalding's name included third on a list of three.

42. George L. Willard to James Cardinal Gibbons, May 7, 1878, Archives of the Archdiocese of Baltimore (hereinafter cited as AAB), printed in Colman Barry, The Catholic Church and the German Americans (Milwaukee, 1952), pp. 46-49.

43. Barry, Catholic Church and German Americans, p. 47.

44. In this province, they were the bishops of St. Paul, Minnesota; Marquette, Michigan; LaCrosse, Wisconsin; Green Bay, Wisconsin; and Fargo, North Dakota.

There were no objections to Spalding except for the fact that he was not German.[45]

As the list made its way to Rome, the tension between the Irish and the German priests of the diocese climaxed in a battle of words in the press. The Catholic Citizen accused the German priests on the seminary staff of secretly petitioning Rome for a German-born coadjutor. "Die Columbia claimed that all this talk of a plot was really an attempt to distract attention from the real conspiracy on the part of the English-speaking Catholics and to end German rule."[46]

The clash escalated to the pages of the Milwaukee Daily News in December of 1878 when the editors of that paper saw fit to comment on the conflict. "The prestige of the Catholic Church will soon be lost," went the editorial, "if her clergy have sunk to the level of political tricksters, if they engage in ecclesiastical wire-pulling and if her hierarchy becomes a Returning Board to seat their favorites in positions of emolument and honor."[47] The battle continued into January 1879 with charge and counter-charge appearing both in the secular and the religious press. There appeared to be no end to the bitterness.[48]

---

45. Barry, Catholic Church and German-Americans, pp. 48-49.

46. Ibid., p. 49; Die Columbia, January 16, 1879; Catholic Citizen, December 21, 1878, January 4, 18, 1879.

47. Milwaukee Daily News, December 18, 22, 25, 29, 1878, January 1, 1879.

48. Milwaukee Daily News, ibid., and January 1, 19, 29, 1879; Milwaukee Sentinel, December 16, 21, 23, 1878; Catholic Citizen, January 4, 18, 25, 1879; Die Columbia, December 26, 1878.

But the battle did end with a strongly worded circular from Archbishop Henni condemning the public agitation and restraining his priests from making further comments. Henni noted that the decision was in the hands of the Pope and that public discussion brought only tension and bitterness to the archdiocese.[49] "Another moderating factor occurred after the death of Martin Kundig on March 9, 1879, in the appointment of Patrick J. Donahue, pastor of the Cathedral, a predominantly Irish parish, to the position of vicar general to succeed Kundig."[50] Donahue was the first non-German administrator in the history of the archdiocese.

The "coadjutor problem," as it was called, did highlight the fragile nature of Henni's diocesan leadership. Even after thirty-three years of peaceful operation in Milwaukee, ethnicity was still a major issue in the archdiocese. The success of the Henni administration lay with the bishop himself rather than his organization. Once he removed himself from the operation, the Catholic community devolved into the fighting so common in Chicago.

Henni's style of episcopal leadership had been effective since the establishment of the Milwaukee diocese in 1844. Yet Bishops Henni and Heiss were never able to overcome the problem of antagonism between Irish and German Catholics. In search of a

---

49. Archbishop Henni to the Priests of the Archdiocese of Milwaukee, January 19, 1879, AAM.

50. M. Justile McDonald, The Irish in Wisconsin in the Nineteenth Century (Washington, 1954), p. 214; Catholic Citizen, March 15, 1879.

permanent solution to the "German question," the Reverend Peter M. Abbelen, a priest in Milwaukee, petitioned the Vatican in 1886 to formally approve the Milwaukee plan of ethnic parishes. The furor created by misinterpretation and misunderstanding of the issue obscured it.[51] By the middle of 1887, the question of preserving the German Catholic identity had become national in scope. Even though the controversy had begun in Milwaukee and the issue was hotly debated in that city, Heiss made no changes in his administration as a result. The operation of the archdiocese continued to reflect an uneasy peace between the Irish and the Germans.

IV

These two dioceses provide contrasting portraits of the dynamics of diocesan leadership in the nineteenth century Midwest. Between 1840 and 1890, the bishops of Chicago and Milwaukee struggled with administrative and leadership problems that evolved from inter-ethnic hostility and parish localism. Yet the two dioceses reflected different experiences. In Chicago, Irish-born bishops wrestled with the French and German Catholics for control of parish property and fought with pastors over episcopal prerogatives for the first twenty-five years of the diocese's existence. Relations improved with the moderate policies of Thomas Foley during the 1870's and were further strengthened by the appointment of Patrick A. Feehan as first Archbishop. In

---

51. Barry, Catholic Church and German Americans, pp. 63-85, 289-312.

Milwaukee, John M. Henni initially avoided inter-ethnic squabbling by establishing a network of ethnic parishes. But his
loosely knit coalition, which had worked for more than thirty
years, fell apart in 1878 when it came time to choose his successor.

The key to the contrast between these two dioceses lies in
an understanding of the sources of authority within the American
Church. Early historians of American Catholicism believed that
the bishops commanded and the clergy and laity obeyed, but this
was not the case in Chicago or Milwaukee. Orderly administration, in these two dioceses at least, demanded a balance of power
between the bishops and the parishes. "The sheer necessity of
building churches at a rate rapid enough to bring the Mass within
reach of the incoming tides of newcomers," notes Sam Bass Warner,
"necessarily delivered much of the power of the organization into
the hands of the parish."[52] Because Thomas Foley and Patrick
Feehan understood this, their tenures contrasted with those of
their predecessors. John Henni also understood this and the very
thought of his retirement put his diocese in chaos until the policies of his successor were known. Throughout most of the nineteenth century, collective decision-making was the hallmark of
the bishop who wished to administer his diocese in peace.

---

52. Sam Bass Warner, The Urban Wilderness (New York, 1972),
p. 163.

CHAPTER IV

THE DIOCESAN CAMPAIGN FOR PARISH SCHOOLS

I

Of all the problems facing American Catholics in the nineteenth century, none was quite so complex as the education of
their children. Many Catholic parents were tempted to send their
children to common schools. But could nominally Protestant or
non-religious institutions be trusted with the intellectual welfare of Catholic children? If not, was it constitutional to
require Catholics to pay taxes for schools that violated their
consciences? Were parish schools the answer to the problem of
protecting the religious faith of Catholic children and at the
same time educating them to be deferential, diligent, productive
Americans? The answers to these questions were not obvious to
Catholic parents in the mid-nineteenth century.[1]

In an effort to convince Catholic parents to spurn public
schools and support parish schools, Church leaders exerted social
pressure on two levels. One "campaign" was conducted on the

---

1. The best survey of Catholic education in the nineteenth
century is Robert D. Cross, "Origins of the Catholic Parochial
Schools in America," American Benedictine Review 16 (June 1965):
194-209. For background on the involvement of the laity in
Catholic education, see Timothy L. Smith, "Parochial Education
and American Culture," in Paul Nash, ed., History and Education
(New York, 1970), pp. 192-211. For citations to studies of
Catholic education in specific cities, see Michael W. Sedlak and
Timothy Walch, American Educational History: A Guide to
Information Sources (Detroit, 1981), pp. 137-143.

parish level. As the most important and visible representatives of the Church in the neighborhoods, parish pastors had at least weekly opportunities, through sermons at Sunday Mass, to cajole and convince their parishioners to choose Catholic education. The impact and effect of this campaign varied dramatically from parish to parish depending on the interest and commitment of individual pastors.

The most successful local campaigns were conducted in the ethnic parishes, particularly those in German and Polish neighborhoods. The school became the focal point for preserving and nurturing ethnic traditions as well as religious faith. The two were interdependent. "Denationalization is demoralization," thundered one German priest. "A foreigner who loses his nationality is in danger of losing his faith and character."[2]

The ethnic parish school was, therefore, an extension of both church and culture. Immigrant parents placed their hope in the school, hope that the sister-teachers would nurture in the children the ethnic traditions that the parents held so dear. When the parish pastor called for funds to support the school, there was no debate. Immigrant parents knew that the parish school was vital to the faith of the next generation.

A second campaign was waged beyond parish boundaries at the diocesan level. Using Catholic newspapers and magazines, Church leaders attacked the immorality of the nominally Protestant com-

---

2. Anton H. Walburg, "The Question of Nationality in its Relation to the Catholic Church," an 1889 pamphlet reprinted in Aaron I. Abell, ed., American Catholic Thought on Social Questions (Indianapolis, 1968), p. 44.

mon schools and castigated Catholic parents who supported these institutions or were lax in their support of parochial schools.

The diocesan campaign for parish schools was not an easy one for the Catholic leadership. Popular notions to the contrary, the laity did not blindly obey the objectives of the bishops and the clergy. Even though parish school enrollments grew substantially throughout the nineteenth century, it is not likely that more than half of the Catholic children in this country ever received a Catholic education. Many Catholic parents from all social classes simply ignored episcopal directives and sent their children to public schools.

The frustration of Catholic school advocates in not being able to convince a majority of the laity to support parish schools is dramatically illustrated in the pages of the Catholic press. Some of the stories claimed that public schools produced shallow, amoral, materialistic graduates; other articles touted parish schools as the bulwark of old-fashioned American values and true religious devotion. Some publications went so far as to fashion fiction that melodramatically contrasted the results of parochial and public school educations. All of the articles were written in a language that seems shrill, overblown, and alarmist by contemporary standards. But one must keep in mind the fact that the purpose of these articles was not to inform or educate, but to pressure the laity to conform to the wishes of the Catholic hierarchy on education.[3]

---

3. For a detailed discussion of the rhetoric of one influential editor, see Thomas T. McAvoy, "Public Schools vs. Catholic Schools and James McMaster," Review of Politics 28 (January

The press campaign to persuade Catholic parents to support parish schools took on different dimensions in different dioceses and varied depending on the educational views of different bishops and editors. Some of the men were dogmatic and condemnatory, others were gentle and conciliatory. All had the common goal of convincing Catholic parents to support parochial schools.

II

Chicago was a diocese in turmoil almost from its establishment in 1843. The first bishop, William Quarter, had barely begun his work when he died suddenly in 1848. Quarter's successor, James G. Van de Velde, quarrelled with priests and laity alike and was never able to exert much influence over the parishes of his diocese. Under such circumstances, it is surprising that Catholics were willing to establish and support nine parochial schools, two orphanages, a female academy, and a university by 1852.

This is not to say that Catholic education flourished during the Van de Velde years, far from it. The nine parochial schools could provide for only a few hundred of the thousands of Catholic children in the diocese. Van de Velde knew that he would have to persuade or perhaps shame the laity into building more schools. Like bishops in other dioceses, he chose a diocesan newspaper as his medium.[4]

1966): 19-46. For an example of melodramatic fiction with a Catholic educational theme, see Mary Anne Sadlier, The Blakes and the Flanagans (New York, 1855).

4. For the history of Catholic education in Chicago in the nineteenth century, see James W. Sanders, The Education of an

Founded early in 1852, The Western Tablet was the voice used
by a small group of Catholic school advocates in Chicago. In the
pages of the Tablet, publisher Daniel O'Hara and editor John
McMullen lashed out at those parents who did not support parish
schools. In an unsigned editorial less than two months after the
paper was founded, McMullen bemoaned the indifference and "cul-
pable neglect" of many Catholic parents in regard to the education of their children. "Numbers of them, chiefly boys," wrote
McMullen, "are suffered to grow up in ignorance -- to run about
the streets and contract low habits which must finally render
them a nuisance to society, a disgrace to their religion, and a
curse to their own careless and guilty parents."[5] McMullen further called for Catholics to express their support for good
"Christian" education. "Religion, clean and undefiled before
God," he wrote, "is the parent of true liberty and patriotism."[6]

Yet the laity did not heed his advice and less than a year
later McMullen cautioned his readers that all too many Chicago
Catholics were sending their children to public schools or to no
school at all. McMullen was well aware that as long as this
situation continued, diocesan leaders would look foolish in their
petitions for state school funds." "Whoever does send his children to the public school," exclaimed an editorial on March 5,
1853, "is weakening our cause by lending help to the enemies of

Urban Minority: Catholics in Chicago, 1833-1965 (New York, 1977),
pp. 18-39, 56-71; and Charles Shanabruch, Chicago's Catholics:
The Evolution of an American Identity (Notre Dame, 1981), pp. 1-
30.

5. The Western Tablet, April 3, 1852.

6. Ibid., March 13, 1852.

Catholicity."[7] The _Tablet_ hoped to shame lax parents into supporting only parochial schools, thus creating a united front in
the Catholic appeal for state school funds.

In a March 19 article entitled "Catholic Education in Illinois -- The Beginning of the End," McMullen went to extraordinary
lengths to emphasize the dangers of public education. Referring
to the common schools as "nurseries of heathenism, vice and
crime," he accused guilty Catholic parents of committing "spiritual murder." Indeed, as the article progressed, McMullen's rhetoric became even more inflammatory. "If your son or daughter is
attending a state school," he cried, "you may be as certain that
you are violating your duty as a Catholic parent and contributing
to the everlasting anguish and despair of your child as if you
could take your oath of it. You ought not be able to rest an in-
stant, to bargain, labor, recreate, eat, drink, sleep with comfort, until you have removed your child from the proximate occasion of spiritual ruin."[8] McMullen concluded by stating that
even illiteracy was preferable to a common school education.

McMullen's threats and warnings to the contrary, Catholic
parents in Chicago continued to support public schools. Without
any evidence of positive results, McMullen abandoned his campaign
for the time being. Catholics in Chicago in the mid-1850s became
preoccupied with a variety of other problems. Late in 1854 the
Tablet folded leaving the diocesan leadership without a voice,
and Van de Velde quit the troubled diocese for the tropical

7. _Ibid._, March 5, 1853.

8. _Ibid._, March 12, 19, 1853.

climes of Natchez, Mississippi. The change in leadership did not bring peace to the diocese, however. "There are serious difficulties in this diocese," wrote the new bishop, Anthony O'Regan, soon after his arrival in Chicago. "I dread to encounter them. Differences here are altogether unlike what I have known elsewhere."[9]

There were two reasons why Catholics in Chicago in the 1850s failed to build parish schools in great numbers. Certainly poverty prevented many of the newest parishioners from establishing and supporting such schools. But another major reason was the tolerant environment some Catholics found in Chicago's public schools. "We have a large number of Catholic children in our schools," noted Superintendent William Wells in 1858, "but I have not during the two and a half years that I have been connected with them heard so much as a suspicion expressed by any quarter that any of the teachers were attempting to exert a sectarian influence."[10] Wells further noted that Catholics were teaching in the public schools and were active on the school board. Even though Bible reading was very much a part of the curriculum, many Catholic parents sent their children to the local public schools throughout the 1850s and 1860s.

After four years of frustration, O'Regan "retired" and left Chicago in 1858. His successor, James Duggan, lasted a decade

9. O'Regan to John M. Henni, November 6, 1854; O'Regan to Richard Purcell, January 26, 1855; O'Regan to Peter R. Kenrick, May 19, 1855; copies in AAC.

10. William H. Wells to I. Haines, December 2, 1858 in the William H. Wells Papers, CHS.

but made little progress in convincing his flock to build parochial schools sufficient for the growing number of Catholic children in the diocese. The Civil War preoccupied Chicago Catholics
as it did other citizens and little was done to build new schools
during that decade. As if to make matters worse, Duggan's gra-
dual mental deterioration and his eventual commitment to an asylum, diverted the attention of Chicago Catholics away from education.[11]

The campaign for more Catholic schools was renewed by
Duggan's successor, Thomas Foley, assisted by the recently or-
dained John McMullen, the former editor of the Tablet. Using a
new diocesan newspaper, The Western Catholic, they renewed the
campaign to obtain a share of the state school fund for Catholic
education and to point out the inadequacies of public education.
The editors of The Western Catholic carefully avoided any comment
on the reluctance of Catholics to build parish schools.

During the mid-1870s, The Western Catholic focused on the
immorality of public education and the importance of religion in
any curriculum in a renewed effort to convince Catholic parents
to support parish schools.[12] In January 1873, The Western
Catholic explored the fundamental purposes of education. "Is it
simply imparting the contents of arithmetics, geographies, and

---

11. For background on the Duggan problem and its effects on
the diocese, see James P. Gaffey, "Patterns of Ecclesiastical
Succession, 1865-1881," Church History 42 (June 1973): 257-271.

12. The Western Catholic, October 19, November 30, 1872.

grammars?" the editors asked.   "Too often religion, which should be the basis of all knowledge, is most sadly neglected."[13]

This particular criticism of public schools may have had some effect on the laity as increasing numbers of Catholic parents chose to send their children to parish schools in the 1870s. The number of Catholic schools in Chicago more than doubled and enrollment increased 80 percent in the years from 1870 to 1875. Yet there were never enough schools to provide a place for every Catholic child in the diocese.   Foley and McMullen were still a long way off from the goal of placing every Catholic child in a parochial school.

For the next decade The Western Tablet was silent on educational matters.   The reasons are unknown, but perhaps the diocesan leadership became convinced that more agitation in the press would do little to rally additional laity to the bosom of the Church.   For whatever reason, it was not until January 1884 that the paper, now under the patronage of Archbishop Patrick A. Feehan, once again took up the question of Catholic parochial education.   The editors chose not to rehash the issues of the past, but rather to focus on the need for a centralized school board for the parochial schools of Chicago.   The editors noted that their objective was "to place Catholic schools not only on an equality with public schools, but also to elevate them to such a standard of efficiency as will make them the objects of envy to our non-Catholic neighbors.   Organization in education can accom-

---

13. Ibid., January 4, 18, April 12, 1873.

plish anything."[14]   But such optimism was not yet warranted in an archdiocese struggling just to build schools.

By the end of 1884, after the Third Plenary Council had mandated the establishment of a Catholic school in every parish, The Western Catholic made a concrete proposal in favor of a statewide board of education for Catholic schools. It is likely that the proposal was a response to the bishops of the province who had earlier called on the laity to "elevate" the quality of Catholic education and to provide for "uniformity" in textbooks used within the province. Feehan and his colleagues climaxed the movement for parochial school reform at the first archepiscopal synod of Chicago in 1887 when he established the first Catholic board of school examiners for the archdiocese.[15]

The middle years of the nineteenth century were decades of turmoil for the Catholic Church in Chicago. Bishops came and went with alarming frequency, giving the diocese a troubled reputation. Adding to the problems was the inability or unwillingness of many Chicago Catholics to support parish schools. Try as they might, using every imaginable argument and threat, diocesan leaders in Chicago could not change the minds of many Catholic parents. By 1885, Archbishop Feehan and his clergy had accepted the fact that not every Catholic child in Chicago would sit in a Catholic classroom and turned their attention to improving the quality of existing Catholic schools.

_____

14. Ibid., February 23, 1884.

15. Sanders, Education of an Urban Minority, 142-143.

III

Only ninety miles to the north, the Diocese of Milwaukee stood in placid contrast to the Diocese of Chicago. Established as a diocese in 1843, the same year as Chicago, Milwaukee did not experience the frequent changes in episcopal leadership or the fractious relations between bishop and laity that so plagued Chicago. For more than thirty-five years the diocese was led by the sure, steady hand of the Swiss-born "diplomat," John Martin Henni. He quietly went about the business of the Church -- building schools, hospitals, and asylums with few of the confrontations that so plagued Chicago.[16]

This is not to say that the laity eagerly established schools in every parish. Indeed, they did not. Just as in Chicago, some Catholics in Milwaukee -- particularly English-speaking Catholics -- were somewhat reluctant to invest their limited funds in parish schools. Michael Heiss noted this problem soon after the diocese was founded. "If our Catholic children are to be instructed in the catechism," he wrote to a friend, "the Catholics have to support their own schools . . . . But not all of our Catholics are zealous enough to make these sacrifices."[17] Heiss was not alone in his concerns. "The laity

---

16. For the history of Catholics and Catholic education in Milwaukee, see Kathleen Neils Conzen, Immigrant Milwaukee, 1836-60: Accommodation and Community in a Frontier City (Cambridge, 1976), pp. 63-74, and Bayard Still, Milwaukee: The History of a City (Madison, 1948).

17. Heiss to George Kellerman, May 23, 1844, original in ASFS, published in Salesianum 9 (1914); Henni to Joseph Mueller, April 24, 1845, ASFS, published in Salesianum 37 (1942).

do not seem willing to entrust us with the young generation upon whom I build my hopes," stated Josef Salzmann. "Attendance at school and interest in educational matters is far from being what I desire."[18] In the early years of the diocese, the English-speaking laity was a source of disappointment for diocesan leaders.

It was the small community of Irish Catholics that most worried Henni, Heiss, and Salzmann. In a city dominated by Germans, the Irish Catholics often had more in common with native Protestants than they did with their fellow Catholics. In fact, most Irish Catholics in Milwaukee sent their children to public schools rather than build their own. How could these Irish Catholics be convinced to support parish schools? It was clear that the bishop needed a "voice" but the English-speaking community in Milwaukee was too small to support a Catholic newspaper for the first twenty-five years of Henni's tenure.

Finally, late in 1869, Henni was able to sponsor The Star of Bethlehem directed at his English-speaking parishioners. The editors wasted no time in outlining the differences between Catholics and non-Catholics on educational matters. "We are well aware that the majority of American minds are incapable of placing a higher value on education than that which pays the way to wealth and fame," went the editorial. "To our mind, education aims not only at the means of producing a wise and well-ordered

18. Salzmann to Michael Hanreidter, October 10, 1849, ASFS; Peter L. Johnson, ed., "The Letters of the Right Reverend Anthony Urbanek," Wisconsin Magazine of History 10 (September 1926): 86-87.

state of citizenship, wherein men act honestly by each other, but also where Christianity and civilization fits a man to so conduct himself that his after-state may be reliably looked upon as one of eternal salvation."[19] The message was a directive to Catholics with children in the public schools: What will it profit your children if they gain wealth and fame but lose their souls?

In the December issue, "Catholicus" initiated a direct attack on the common schools. A variety of ills concerned the author in his front page story: "The common school system violates the right of every Christian denomination by preventing, to some extent, the members thereof from educating their children according to their religious principles and convictions. This right is given by the Creator to the parents and no state can justly usurp this natural guardianship . . . . We can never be convinced that Protestant teachers, nursed in prejudice against the Catholic Church, will give impartial judgement upon Catholic concerns. The common schools are the means of propagating slanders against Catholics and Catholicism throughout the whole country."[20]

"Catholicus" capsulized all of the grievances of the Catholic clergy and the Catholic Church against the common schools. Yet the harsh nature of the article, in a newspaper read almost exclusively by Irish Catholics, was clearly directed at Catholic parents who sent their children to public schools. "Catholicus" hoped to exert some moral pressure on these "lax" Catholics.

---

19. The Star of Bethlehem 1 (November 1869).

20. Ibid., 1 (December 1869).

In March 1871, The Star of Bethlehem merged into a new diocesan paper, The Catholic Vindicator, and the name captured its
tone. In one of its first issues, the paper perceived a wide influence for Catholic schooling. "It would be difficult to con-
ceive of a system of education," went the editorial, "better cal-
culated to promote the best interests of society and mutual
social relations for the greater good and consequently the best
interest and happiness of the state."[21]

Yet the editors never lost sight of the principal functions
of parochial schools -- to preserve the faith and culture of
Catholicism. The editors of The Catholic Vindicator went so far
as to link the very survival of the Catholic Church in America to
the existence of parish schools. "Catholics are violating a most
sacred duty," concluded the editors at the end of 1871, "in not
providing facilities for Catholic education." He called on the
laity to "cast off its lethargy" and to discard the "flimsy arguments of liberal Catholicism" and "make their voices heard" in
favor of Catholic schooling.[22]

But The Catholic Vindicator was unable to rally Milwaukee's
English-speaking Catholics to support parish schools and by the
end of the decade a new diocesan newspaper, The Catholic Citizen,
had replaced the Vindicator. The Catholic Citizen was a no-
nonsense paper that went right to the heart of the problem. "The
majority of persons in Catholic congregations," wrote the editors, "have no pride in their school. It is regarded with toler-

21. The Catholic Vindicator, March 2, 1871.

22. Ibid., December 28, 1871, January 25, 1872.

ation as a lobby of the pastor and his dutiful people are always eager on the slightest pretext to send their children to a public school."[23]   The Citizen was disgusted with Milwaukee's English-speaking Catholic community.

In March of 1879, the Citizen announced an innovative incentive for the laity to build parish schools. An anonymous donor agreed to give one hundred dollars, a substantial sum at the time, to any parish in Milwaukee that established a new school provided that the schoolhouse was built of brick or stone, accommodated at least seventy-five pupils, and that classes were taught in the English language. By the end of 1879 not one parish had accepted the offer, a state of affairs that angered the Citizen. "Are there no congregations," the editors asked "where there are children enough to make a school yet at present have no school? Certainly there are such congregations. This shows that the people are not as much in earnest as they should be in regard to this subject."[24]

The Citizen also castigated the laity who sent their children to public schools. "They live where Catholic schools are already established and are conducted in the best manner. Yet they send their children to the public schools. Such parents can scarcely be called Catholics." The Citizen spoke of the Catholic parish without a school as a "spiritual wilderness."[25]

---

23. The Catholic Citizen, February 8, 1879.

24. Ibid., March 1, 8, December 20, 1879.

25. Ibid., December 20, 1879.

The resistance of the English-speaking Catholics of Milwaukee to the establishment of parish schools was due to two principal reasons. In the parishes without schools, laymen were unwilling to undertake the heavy financial burden of a school, with or without the contribution of a hundred dollars. A second group of Catholics saw parish schools as clearly inferior to their public counterparts and an unnecessary limitation on the futures of their children. Together these recalcitrant parishioners constituted a troublesome and sizable faction in Catholic educational affairs in Milwaukee.

Late in 1882, the _Citizen_ renewed its efforts to promote the value of parochial education. This time the paper tried another traditional approach -- a contrast of the parish school and the public school. "The parish school," went the critique, "is governed by the clergyman, always a man of intelligence who sustains the secular authority of the teacher by the stronger sanction of his sacred character. In the public school the teacher often dares not to reprove the refractory pupil because he is the son or cousin of the trustee, or his father has influence with him or the school inspector. How the teacher trembles when the inspector comes around if there is no _entente cordiale_ between them!"[26] In a follow-up article the next week, the _Citizen_ criticized the public schools for treating students as members of different social classes rather than as individuals.[27]

---

26. _Ibid._, August 26, 1882.

27. _Ibid._, September 3, 1882.

The _Citizen_'s criticism of the public schools was untypical of the paper's commentary on educational matters in the 1880s. Just as _The Western Catholic_ had done in Chicago, _The Catholic Citizen_ focused on improving the quality of Catholic education as a means of attracting more students. Repeatedly throughout the decade, the _Citizen_ called on the Milwaukee Catholic community to make the parochial schools more efficient, raise academic standards, increase the pay of teachers, and above all make the parish schools fully competitive with the public schools. The keystone of these improvements, in the mind of the _Citizen_, was the establishment of a school board. The board would insure that Catholic parish schools continued to meet the highest standards.[28]

The actions taken at the Third Plenary Council in 1884 reinforced the program of educational reform previously outlined in the pages of _The Catholic Citizen_. At the time of the publication of the decrees, the editors of the Milwaukee paper applauded the wisdom of the assembled bishops. The decrees stated clearly that every parish must establish and maintain a school except under special circumstances. Perhaps now, argued the editors, recalcitrant Catholic parents would do their duty and support parish schools.[29]

But thirty years of prayer and fifteen years of rhetoric in the Milwaukee Catholic press did not dissipate the alienation of many Irish Catholics from the German-dominated Church in their

28. _Ibid._, August 25, 1883; May 3, June 14, 1884.

29. _Ibid._, December 20, 1884.

hometown.   Even the proclamations of the assembled bishops at Baltimore had little effect.   These Catholic parents continued to send their children to public schools in spite of all threats and pleadings.   By 1885, diocesan leaders grudgingly acknowledged this fact and turned their attention to building parish schools among the Germans and Poles.

IV

The campaign for parish schools during the middle years of the nineteenth century was an uphill struggle for the American Catholic Church.   Catholic leaders had to raise the funds to build the classrooms and find the teachers to staff them.   More importantly, the bishops and other diocesan leaders had to convince many -- perhaps the majority -- of the laity of the need for separate schools.   Using the Catholic press and the pulpit, Catholic leaders in many dioceses mounted campaigns to praise the value of Catholic schooling and warn of the dangers of public education.   As the case studies of Chicago and Milwaukee suggest, the results of these campaigns were mixed.   In spite of thirty years of propaganda, many Catholic parents continued to send their children to public schools.

To be sure, the establishment of Catholic parochial schools in the nineteenth century was a success by almost any standard. Beginning in the 1840s with a handful of classrooms and a few hundred students, Catholic parochial schools grew to 2,500 institutions and nearly half a million students nation-wide by 1885. This was an exceptional achievement.   Indeed, the establishment of Catholic parochial schools must be ranked as one of the most impressive social movements in American history.

In spite of this achievement, diocesan leaders were disappointed that the campaign fell so far short of the stated goal of enrolling every Catholic child in a Catholic school. Never more than half of the Catholic children in the United States ever enrolled in parish schools. During the years after the Third Plenary Council, Catholic leaders gradually accepted the fact that their goal was unrealistic and turned their attention to improving the quality of existing parish schools and to establishing new schools among that portion of the laity interested in Catholic education.

CHAPTER V

PARISH PASTORS AND PAROCHIAL EDUCATION

I

The establishment and operation of Catholic parochial schools was a collaborative effort. Many Catholics -- bishops, parents, and teachers -- made important contributions to the form and content of Catholic education. Yet no contribution was greater or more important than that of parish pastors. In fact, it was parish pastors who determined the final outcome of the campaign for parish schools. Bishops called for schools; the laity contributed money and labor; nuns contributed their considerable classroom skills. But without the active support of parish pastors, these contributions would not have meant very much. The pastors raised the monies, built the schoolhouses, recruited the teachers, established the curriculum, and enrolled the students. In sum, they were the sine qua non of parochial education in the nineteenth century.

The pastor's involvement in education was an extension of his dual role as minister of the gospel and neighborhood leader. As minister of the gospel, the pastor obviously was concerned about the spiritual welfare of Catholic children. As neighborhood leader, he also was concerned about the material welfare and economic future of these same young Catholics. For many pastors, the answer to both concerns was the parish school. It was a social institution that served both a spiritual and a temporal purpose.

Yet pastoral support for parish schools was far from universal. Some pastors were parochial education enthusiasts. German and Polish pastors, concerned that their children would become "Anglicized" and lose their religious faith in the public schools, quickly established parish schools. Other pastors were less enthusiastic and some pastors were even hostile to parochial education. Some Irish pastors, for example, had mixed feelings about such institutions. "Many priests were simply 'irresolute,'" notes Robert Cross, "always hoping for some accommodation with the state that would relieve the people and themselves from carrying, unaided, the burden of formal education."[1]

The ambivalence of these pastors was not the result of a crisis of faith. Rather it was a reflection of the substantial burden caused by the operation of a parish school. "Financially, the parish school was a drain on the church;" notes Jay P. Dolan, "one priest, exasperated with his debts, closed the school and marched the children to the local public school where he arranged for their admission."[2] The burden would have been easier to bear if the laity had been more generous in their support. But many Catholic parents also found the cost of parish education to be burdensome. "We can bear the burden no longer," one group of

----

1. Robert D. Cross, "The Origins of Catholic Parochial Schools in America," American Benedictine Review 16 (June 1965): 204.

2. Jay P. Dolan, Immigrant Church: New York's Irish and German Catholics, 1815-1865 (Baltimore, 1975), p. 109.

laymen told their archbishop. "My God, what can we do?"[3] For some the cost was too high and public schools were the only alternative.

In spite of these problems, the majority of pastors, Irish as well as German, made sincere efforts to establish and maintain parish schools. On balance, most parish pastors believed education to be far too important to be left to chance. The objective of the parish school was "to transmit the values of Catholic culture to younger generations and to reinforce the more informal education offered in the church and the home. As an ethnic institution, it also aimed at preserving a national heritage that was in danger of being lost in a new environment."[4] The lack of schoolhouses, the appeal of public schools, the insufficient financial resources, and the resistance of some parents all limited the growth of parochial education. But under no circumstances did any or all of these factors undermine the general commitment of parish pastors to the operation of parochial schools.

Who were these men? They were a motley collection of missionary and diocesan clergy, both foreign- and American-born. They were a generation of individuals who applied the gospel in their own individual ways. As different as they were from one another, they all shared an intense religious faith that carried them through years of sacrifice and hard work. But beyond such brief statements, it is hard to generalize about these priests.

---

3. Cross, "Origins of Catholic Parochial Schools," p. 202.

4. Dolan, Immigrant Church, p. 111.

They were men of action who left behind few manuscripts or memoirs of their ministries. As a result they generally have been ignored in the history of American education.[5]

Even though it is difficult to evaluate these pastors as a group, it is possible to present selected case studies of individual priests. The lives of Arnold Damen, S.J., of Chicago and Martin Kundig of Milwaukee were both typical and untypical of the lives of average pastors. Both men were leaders in their respective dioceses, yet their experiences also provide informative perspectives on parochial school development on the local level. The stories of Damen and Kundig, variations of which were played out in thousands of parishes across the nation, underscore the importance of the parish pastors in the nineteenth century Catholic educational experience.

II

When the Jesuits came to Chicago in 1857 and established Holy Family parish on the city's west side, they initiated one of the most extraordinary educational enterprises in the history of

5. The historical literature on the American Catholic priesthood has improved substantially in recent years. The foremost work on these men is John Tracy Ellis, ed., The Catholic Priest in the United States: Historical Investigations (Collegeville, MN, 1971). A useful case study of one diocese is Donna Merwick, Boston Priests, 1848-1910: A Study of Social and Intellectual Change (Boston, 1973). Jay P. Dolan's Catholic Revivalism: The American Experience, 1830-1900 (Notre Dame, 1977) is an exceptional study of the impact of missionary priests on the spiritual development of parishes. Another useful work is Ellen Skerrett's The Irish Parish in Chicago, 1880-1930, Cushwa Center Working Papers Series (Notre Dame, 1981). These studies are only a beginning, however; much more work on the priesthood remains to be done.

the city. The key to their success was Arnold Damen, who proved
to be a dynamic orator, a forceful administrator, and most important of all, an effective fund raiser. By 1877, Damen's parish
had grown beyond all known proportions. Enrollment figures for
the 1870s and 1880s indicate that just three of its five schools
were educating nearly 30 percent of all of the children enrolled
in Catholic schools in Chicago during those decades.

Damen was born in Belgium in 1815. He became convinced of
his religious vocation to the priesthood and the American missions after hearing a sermon by the famous Jesuit missionary,
Pierre-Jean DeSmet. Damen traveled with DeSmet, and other re-
cruits to St. Louis in the late 1830s and after ordination, he
devoted his life to preaching missions throughout the Middle
West. Damen was considered one of the most powerful Catholic
preachers of his time.[6]

Damen's involvement with Chicago can be traced to a simple
invitation by Bishop Anthony O'Regan to the Jesuits to conduct a
mission for the Catholics of Chicago in August of 1856. In response to this routine request, the Jesuit provincial superior
sent Damen and three other priests to conduct the service. To
say that the mission was successful is something of an understatement. Contemporary newspaper accounts reported that 12,000

6. As with many priests, Damen awaits a scholarly biographer.
The most complete information can be found in Gilbert J.
Garraghan, Jesuits of the Middle United States (3 vols., New
York, 1938). Dolan, Catholic Revivalism, includes useful infor-
mation on Damen's skills as an orator. Also see Skerrett, The
Irish Parish in Chicago, pp. 8-9. The only biography to date has
been Joseph Conroy, Arnold Damen: A Chapter in the Making of
Chicago (New York, 1930).

Catholics received communion on a single day, and that no combination of churches could accommodate "the multitude that crowded from all parts of the city."[7] It was a religious event without precedent in Chicago.

The mission convinced O'Regan that he had to have a Jesuit parish in his diocese. "I know of no better work for religion," wrote O'Regan, "for the diocese or for my own soul than establishing here a house for your society and this is the reason that I have been so anxious to effect this. It was on this account as also from my personal regard and affection for your institute as for many of your Fathers individually, that I so urgently tried to see this good work accomplished."[8] The resulting agreement assigned Damen to establish the city's first Jesuit parish.

The location of the new parish was a point of contention between O'Regan and Damen. The bishop wanted to establish the Jesuits in the heart of what was then a stockyard district, but Damen objected. He had done his own survey of the area and found less than a dozen Catholic families. In writing to his superiors in St. Louis, Damen noted that O'Regan "still continues recommending this place and says that we will regret it; but I cannot believe that, informed as I am about the few Catholic families in the vicinity."[9] Damen selected a piece of property on the city's

---

7. Harry C. Koenig, ed., A History of the Parishes of the Archdiocese of Chicago (2 vols., Chicago, 1980), 1:367.

8. O'Regan to Damen, October 1856, SLUA, published in Garraghan, Jesuits, 3:396; O'Regan to Damen, March 21, 1857, SLUA, in Garraghan, Jesuits, 3:397.

9. Quoted in Koenig, History of Chicago Parishes, 1:369

west side, in an area being settled by Bohemian, German, and Irish immigrants. "Here we will have a large Catholic population at once," noted Damen, "sufficient to fill a large church."[10]

Damen was a man of big plans. Soon after the formal establishment of the parish in early May 1857, the Chicago Daily Journal reported that "the Order of Jesuits has resolved to establish a church, college, and free school on a scale of magnitude equal to any of the same character in the United States."[11] This was an extraordinary claim, coming as it did when Chicago was in the midst of a financial depression. But Damen threw himself into the project. A temporary church was dedicated in July and the cornerstone for the permanent church was laid in August. By September, Damen had opened both a school for boys and one for girls. He was a priest on the move!

But big plans cost big money and Damen found the bishop to be a poor man. In response to Damen's request for monetary support, O'Regan wrote that "as to the resources you suppose me to have -- I have no such, as I think you must know. You are aware how much we are in debt and how much must be expended before any revenue can be derived from our churches."[12] O'Regan's poverty forced Arnold Damen to become the most effective fund raiser in the city. Damen's leadership in this area allowed him to expand his parish beyond all expectations.

---

10. Ibid.

11. Chicago Daily Journal, May 19, 1857.

12. O'Regan to Damen, October 1856, in Garraghan, Jesuits 3:396.

Damen labored under the same handicaps as other parish pastors in the city. He initially collected money for his schools
by going door-to-door in the neighborhoods adjacent to his parish. The response was mixed. A parishioner who joined Damen on
one such excursion related the story of a wealthy businessman who
would not give money for the support of "frogs and wild ducks," a
reference to the marshes that made up a substantial part of the
parish at that time. After repeated cajoling, he finally gave
Damen a dollar. "I shook my head at the Father not to take the
amount," wrote the parishioner, "but he did and thanked the
giver. 'O Father!' I said when we reached the sidewalk, 'why did
you take that paltry dollar?' 'My good friend,' said Damen,
'every little helps.'"[13]

Damen also sought money from his superiors in St. Louis.
"Please send me the remainder of the money from the festival," he
wrote in June 1858, "for I have a great many payments." The
following month he asked his superiors "to act cleverly for
Chicago" and send him six thousand dollars in payment for a certain piece of real estate. He promised that he would never ask
for money again, but he did not keep his word. Damen continued
to seek money from his provincial superiors as well as from other
sources.[14]

Damen did much more than raise money for his schools, of
course. He also took an active interest in the selection of a

13. James J. McGovern, Souvenir of the Silver Jubilee in the
Episcopacy of Patrick A. Feehan (Chicago, 1891), pp. 192-193.

14. Damen to Father Beckx, May 20, 24, 1859, SLUA, cited in
Garraghan, Jesuits, 3:407.

teaching staff. Although he was fortunate to have several fellow Jesuits to teach the boys, he also needed lay teachers to fill other teaching positions in his rapidly growing school system.

In June 1858 he informed his superiors that he had opened two schools the previous year and had already enrolled three hundred children.[15] To handle the influx he hired three sisters -- Mary, Sarah, and Margaret Ghent, "to conduct choir, play the organ, and teach school for females."[16] He also engaged one Mr. Seaman to assist the Jesuits. "The boy's school costs nothing," he wrote to his superiors, "except for the board of Mr. Seaman; he does remarkably well, keeps excellent order, and is sacristan; he is willing and humble; what he gets from the school goes toward the payment of his debts."[17] From these small beginnings grew Holy Family School which educated over 1,500 students each year from 1865 to 1880.

During the 1860s the corps of teachers swelled with Damen's single-handed recruitment of the Sisters of Charity of the Blessed Virgin Mary, known popularly as the "BVMs." Damen promised the nuns that he would provide a furnished house and an annual salary of $250 for each sister.[18] As Thomas Mulkerins rela-

---

15. Damen to Beckx, August 1858, SLUA, cited in Garraghan, Jesuits, 3:407.

16. Damen to Beckx, June 16, 1858, SLUA, cited in Garraghan, Jesuits; "Beginning of Holy Family Parish in Chicago," Illinois Catholic Historical Review 1 (April 1919): 453.

17. Damen to Beckx, June 16, 1858, SLUA, cited in Garraghan, Jesuits, 3:406.

18. Gilbert Garraghan, The Catholic Church in Chicago, 1637-1871 (Chicago, 1921), p. 204; The New World, April 14, 1900.

ted in his parish history, Damen was anxious to reach an agreement before the beginning of the 1867 school year, explaining to
Father John Donaghue, priest-counselor of the BVM order, "If we
commence about a month before the public schools . . . we will
secure all our Catholic children." He instructed Donaghue that
"We would like to get nine Sisters, but try to send three or four
at once if possible and let them be good teachers, so as to make
a good impression, for the first impression is usually the
lasting one."[19]

Nine sisters arrived in August and on the nineteenth of that
month two new schools, St. Aloysius and St. Stanisalus, opened
their doors to 650 pupils. The establishment of other schools in
Holy Family parish soon followed and by 1870 their combined
enrollment neared 5,000 -- ten times the number of students who
attended the public schools within the parish boundaries.

Small wonder then that the reputation of Arnold Damen and
his Holy Family parish soon spread throughout the city. When
George Phillips published his book Chicago and Her Churches in
1868, Damen was recognized as a leader of the Church in Chicago
and received equal treatment with the bishop, James Duggan.
James J. Sheahan's Chicago Views (1866) had already hailed Damen
as a "Catholic Hercules."[20]

19. Damen to John Donaghue, July 2, 1867 and Donaghue to
Mother Clarke, July 19, 1867, both printed in In the Early Days:
Pages from the Annals of the Sisters of Charity of the Blessed
Virgin Mary (St. Louis, 1919), p. 204.

20. George S. Phillips, Chicago and Her Churches (Chicago,
1868), pp. 534-538; James W. Sheahan, Chicago Views (Chicago,
1866).

Damen's school system became the model for other parishes in the city, but few pastors had Damen's fund-raising abilities and in most parishes the operation of parochial schools was a financial burden. Yet the number of schools in the diocese rose to fifteen by the end of the 1860s, evidence of a serious commitment to education on the part of many pastors.

Educational financing continued to be a problem in the 1870s. Many schools survived because most of the nuns who served as teachers received only room and board for their services. A number of Catholic schools operated on a sliding tuition scale based on the ability of the parents to pay. Fees ranged from fifty cents to a dollar a month depending on the child's course of study, but the children of impoverished families could attend free of charge.

A feature story on Damen's schools that appeared in the Chicago Post and Mail in April 1876 described how the system worked. "From accurate calculations and long experience," noted the report, "it is estimated by the managers of these schools, that the extra tuition collected from those who pay over fifty cents a month is equal to the amount that would be due from non-paying pupils if they were charged at the rate of fifty cents, and as these schools are self supporting, the estimate is based on years of careful observation and practical experiments shows that under the parochial school system the Catholics all educate their children at the rate of $5.50 a year."[21] Yet the total

---

21. Chicago Post and Mail, April 20, 1876.

amount collected from tuition payments, even in Holy Family parish, scarcely met all the expenses of operating the schools.

Some parishes like Holy Family organized Sunday School Associations as a means of raising money for the parish schools. After dividing the parish into school districts, members of the association -- usually parents of school children -- collected an extra dollar per parish family. In Holy Family parish they also distributed the Sunday School Messenger to keep both parents and children informed of the educational activities of the parish.[22]

Such activities provided some assistance to Damen and he welcomed parental involvement in school affairs. Yet at times it was also necessary to prod the laity and keep them mindful of their duties. In May 1873, the editors of the Western Catholic complained the "the whole burden of the work is for the most part thrown upon the clergy who are frequently left to build the school, procure the scholars, and then maintain the teachers. This is far from being right, and it is hoped that Catholic parents will henceforth evince a greater interest in this important work; let them use their means, their time, their influence, and do everything they can to aid the clergy in their noble effort."[23]

In spite of these problems, Damen continued to expand his parish school system. He added two new schools in the 1870s and increased enrollments substantially by the end of the decade. In

---

22. Thomas M. MUlkerins, Holy Family Parish: Priests and People (Chicago, 1925), pp. 458-459.

23. Western Catholic, May 31, 1873.

making his educational enterprise a model for the rest of the city, Damen was fortunate to be supported by a number of fellow Jesuit priests who assumed many of the pastoral duties of the parish.

By 1877 Damen had fulfilled the promises he had made twenty years earlier. He had built a church, a school system, and a college of national reputation. In fact, he had done much more. But by 1877 Damen was looking to the future and other assignments. In that year he took on other responsibilities and left his beloved Holy Family parish. He died on the first day of 1890 while in retirement at Creighton University in Omaha, Nebraska.

Damen was an extraordinary pastor and educator, but many other Chicago priests shared some of his success in establishing and maintaining parish schools. During the 1870s alone the number of schools nearly tripled and enrollments increased by almost ninety percent. The credit for this growth in the Catholic school establishment goes to the dozens of little-known "Father Damens" who also served as pastors of nineteenth-century Chicago parishes.

III

In the early days of 1859, Martin Kundig, Vicar General of the Diocese of Milwaukee, assumed additional responsibilities as pastor of St. John's, the cathedral parish. He was to remain both vicar general and pastor until his death more than twenty years later. Because of his visibility as a diocesan official and confidant of Bishop Henni, it is easy to overlook Kundig's contribution to the cathedral parish.

In many ways Kundig's greatest challenges and contributions to Catholicism in Milwaukee came in his capacity as pastor. During his tenure he officiated at about half of the baptisms held at the cathedral and performed over three hundred marriages during that same time span.   "There was hardly anyone in the cathedral parish who had not felt the benefit of his counsel, presence or purse," noted the parish historian Daniel J. O'Hearn. "To the poor, sick, and unfortunate, he was a true father and friend.   The sinful knelt at his feet and arose strong in resolution to lead better lives; the heartbroken came to him and found ready sympathy."[24]   In sum, Kundig was priest of the people.

Martin Kundig was a member of a generation of missionaries who came to the United States from all over Europe.   Born in Switzerland in 1805, he emigrated to Cincinnati in 1828 in the company of his close friend and fellow countryman, John Martin Henni.   After ordination in 1829, Kundig began the ministry of a missionary across Ohio, Michigan, and Wisconsin.   He founded parishes in southern Ohio, served as superintendent of a county poor house in Michigan, opened the first public school in Wisconsin, and was selected to serve as one of the first regents of the University of Wisconsin.   The majority of his pastoral work took

---

24. Daniel J. O'Hearn, Fifty Years at St. John's Cathedral, 1847-1897 (Milwaukee, 1897), p. 75.

place in the sprawling diocese of Milwaukee that was headed by his friend, John Henni.[25]

Of all his many and varied pastoral activities, Kundig placed a high priority on education. As with most priests of his generation, he was deeply committed to a school in every parish. Time and again he preached the fundamental importance and purpose of Catholic schools -- to insure the preservation of the precious Catholic faith of his people. "Education," Kundig noted in one sermon, "involved as it is in the very idea of a religion such as ours, cannot be a strange work at any time in the hands of a Catholic people . . . . Catholicism addresses itself directly to the heart and conscience of the individual . . . . The religion which numbers baptism and penance among its sacraments cannot be neglectful of the soul's training; the creed which opens and resolves into so majestic and so living a theology, cannot but subserve the cultivation of the intellect."[26] This commitment to the intellect on the past of the Church was embodied in the local parish school.

Kundig was second to no pastor in his commitment to Catholic education. Shortly after his arrival in Milwaukee in 1842, Kundig organized a motley collection of Catholics into St. Peter's parish. "He knew that good Catholics are not necessarily good parishioners," notes Peter Leo Johnson, "and so he made haste to make them synonymous. At once, like magic, arose

---

25. Kundig's life and ministry is covered in Peter Leo Johnson, Stuffed Saddlebags: The Life of Martin Kundig, Priest, 1805-1879 (Milwaukee, 1942).

26. Kundig, "Sermon Book A," p. 38, AAM.

schools, Sunday schools, and societies for financing and caring for the church, its sanctuary, and the promotion of temperance."[27] Kundig opened both a boys school and a girls school in the fall of 1842. Classes were held in the basement of the new church and the teachers were lay people well known to Kundig in his mission work.

But Kundig did not have time to nurture and guide his new parish schools because extensive pastoral responsibilities took him to other parts of southeastern Wisconsin. His commitment to parish schools never waned, however, as he went about establishing schools in tandem with many of the twenty-two parishes he founded in the 1840s. After seven years on the road, Kundig returned to Milwaukee to serve as vicar general of the diocese. In this new position he was concerned about parochial education in all parishes of the diocese.

Kundig was so committed to the establishment of parochial education in his new diocese that he convinced his three sisters to leave their native Switzerland and migrate to Milwaukee to teach school. Beginning in 1854, and for two decades thereafter, Elizabeth, Frances, and Katherine Kundig ran small schools in several locations around what is now metropolitan Milwaukee. The bulk of the teaching was done by Frances, who placed a heavy emphasis on catechism and prayers as well as the "three R's."[28] Discipline was handled by Elizabeth Kundig.

---

27. Johnson, Stuffed Saddlebags, p. 178.

28. Ibid., pp. 249-250.

There is no doubt that the Kundig sisters made an impression on their young charges. Writing more than twenty-five years after the experience, one student vividly recalled his time at one of the Kundig schools. "Miss Frances Kundig sat at the long table and boys and girls gathered round her," remembered John C. Burke, "and amidst the deepest silence she spoke on the history of the Passion. It was not considered a proper thing to ask permission to get a drink of water on those afternoons, and in fact, the urchin who did so was warned promptly by the others that it was Friday."[29]

Burke also remembered the disciplinary techniques used by sister Elizabeth. "There she sat in her arm chair, a tall gaunt woman dressed in black, her face extremely pale and emaciated. She waited in silence for the defense of the offenders, if there was any and after administering some sound advice, she dismissed them."[30] Although they were sisters of the vicar general, the Kundigs received no special treatment -- their schools were typical of parochial establishments in Milwaukee in the mid-nineteenth century.

In 1859 Martin Kundig settled down as pastor of St. John's Cathedral parish. It was to be a frustrating tenure for this builder-priest. As a missionary Kundig had established an untold number of schools, but as a pastor he found the process to be arduous. His responsibilities as vicar general, his lack of

---

29. O'Hearn, Fifty Years at St. John's Cathedral, p. 175.

30. Ibid.

funds, the Civil War, and resistance from the laity all contributed to his frustration.

It was not until 1869 that Kundig was able to begin a building campaign at St. John's. In that he year he proposed the construction of a "bishop's hall" to honor Bishop Henni; the building was to serve as a parish school and place to hold diocesan meetings. The plan was opposed by parishioners, however, who countered with a proposal to establish a small parish school in a private residence near the cathedral. It was the laity and not Kundig who won the day; the home was purchased and refitted as a school.[31]

Even though he now had his school, Kundig was less than satisfied. It was clear to him, if not to a majority of his flock, that a permanent schoolhouse and parish hall were needed. He continued to work toward that goal and plans were ready by 1872. Construction began that year, but it was halted shortly thereafter by the financial depression of 1873. Pressed for funds, parishioners quickly lost what little enthusiasm they had for their project. "Actually in the past there had been grumbling about bearing certain diocesan loads which the parish felt ought to have been born by the diocese," adds Peter Johnson, "and now when the school plans included a hall for general diocesan users, parishioners objected."[32]

Rumors circulated about Kundig's dual role as administrator of diocesan as well as parish funds. Many thought that he was

---

31. Johnson, Stuffed Saddlebags, pp. 251-252

32. Ibid.

supporting the diocese at the expense of the parish. So little progress had been made by June of 1877 that Henni made a personal appeal to the parishioners to retire the debt on the school and the hall. The debt was finally paid off by the end of the decade, but not until Kundig was desperate enough to try lotteries and other questionable fund-raising schemes. Perhaps the parishioners of St. John's finally took pity on the plight of their parish pastor.

Kundig died in 1879 after seven long years of planning, building, and paying for his parish school and parish hall. He was not the only parish pastor who bore such a burden, nor was he the only Milwaukee priest committed to parochial education. During the 1870s in Milwaukee, the number of parish schools nearly tripled and enrollment more than doubled. Expansion during the last half of the decade, after the depression had abated, was extraordinary. Perhaps the struggle of Martin Kundig, a much beloved priest, was an inspiration to other pastors. Whatever the reason, statistics show startling growth in Milwaukee parochial schooling in the 1870s.

IV

In 1911, in the very first volume of the Catholic Educational Review, the rector of the Catholic University of America published a tribute to the role of the parish pastor in parochial education. "The pastor is the regularly appointed agency by which the Church carries on her teaching; the sanctuary is his school," wrote Thomas Shahan. "He is not merely connected

with, or interested in education; his daily and hourly ministra-
tions make him in a very literal sense, a teacher with the most
vital knowledge to impart and the most perfect method of imparting it."[33]   These comments might well be a eulogy for Arnold
Damen, Martin Kundig, and the thousands of other nineteenth century priests who labored to establish a parochial school system
in the United States.

Shahan's comments were no mere lip service. Damen, Kundig,
and their colleagues were, in fact, educators in the fundamental
meaning of the word. Anxious about the future of their religion
in a Protestant society, Catholic pastors devoted themselves to
educational programs of all sorts for Catholics of all ages. The
annual parish mission was, for example, one of the several adult
education enterprises sponsored by the Church.

Yet it was the parish school that absorbed the pastor's time
and financial resources; it was his pride and his preoccupation.
Eventually the time and the energy required to maintain parochial
schools that were competitive with their public counterparts
exceeded the abilities of all but the most energetic priests. By
the end of the century, pastors in a majority of American dioceses had surrendered significant educational responsibilities to
diocesan school boards. Such action was taken in the name of
economy, uniformity, and most importantly, competition with the
public schools. In spite of this transition of authority, the

---

33. Thomas J. Shahan, "The Pastor and Education," The Catholic
Educational Review 1 (January, 1911): 40.

educational role of the pastor continued well into the twentieth century.

CHAPTER VI

THE EXPERIENCES OF SISTER TEACHERS

I

No group made greater sacrifices for Catholic parochial
education than did the women religious of the nineteenth century.
The thousands of sister-teachers who staffed parish classrooms
across the country devoted their lives to the children of the
Church. They worked long hours, teaching classes with as many as
100 students, all for subsistence wages. There is no doubt that
the parish school system in this country could never have grown
as large as it did without these sister-teachers. They constituted a "living endowment" that made possible a national system of
parochial schools.[1]

The achievement of these nuns is even more extraordinary
when one considers the obstacles that they faced in this country.
Many of these sisters were born in Europe and were called to the
American missions without much preparation. In fact, they arrived in this country as impoverished as the laity they would
serve. Wretchedly housed and poorly fed in their new dioceses,
most congregations were forced by necessity to dispense with the

---

1. The historiography of Catholic women religious is very
limited. The best volumes on the subject are Mary Ewens, The
Role of the Nun in Nineteenth Century America (New York, 1978)
and Sister Bertrande Meyers, The Education of Sisters (New York,
1941).

more contemplative aspects of their religious rule. Their's was a hard life marked by frequent illness and premature death. Yet it was a life made bearable by the strong religious faith of these women.[2]

As teachers, their lives were made more arduous by the fact that there were few religious or educational traditions within the immigrant Catholic community in the United States. Most Catholics were not only illiterate, they also were ignorant of the tenets of their Faith. To say that the sisters faced a challenge is something of an understatement. "Their pupils differed in racial origin, in social standing, and in financial rating, and their pride of country was a rival to their love of the Church."[3]

Yet these women accepted these realities as an opportunity from God. "Wisely the [religious] Communities adapted themselves, their postulants, and their novices to these conditions, which meant very largely dispensing with professional and preservice training in the Novitiate. A course in general methods sometimes initiated the novice into the problems that she could expect to meet in her work; but most of her professional training was acquired by learning to do by doing."[4] This was to remain the state of affairs in Catholic teacher training well into the twentieth century.

---

2. Meyers, Education of Sisters, pp. 3-21.

3. Ibid., p. 7.

4. Ibid.

To be sure, all religious orders paid lip service to the need for better teacher training, but the general poverty of the Church, the high priority given to the cultivation of religious vocations, and the ever increasing demand for sister-teachers, militated against the establishment of formal teacher preparation programs. It was a frequently stated assumption that divine inspiration would guide the apprentice sister-teacher in the classroom.

The major reason for the lack of classroom preparation was the high priority assigned to the cultivation of religious vocations. "The Communities," notes Sister Bertrande Meyers, "faced with the double task of inducting the young applicant to the religious life and later to the professional, devoted the brief time they were able to retain the candidate at the Mother House to intensive preparation in the religious life and in community customs, trusting that the vocation which called her to 'come' would, if the foundation of a strong spiritual edifice were laid, enable her to 'do.'"[5] This confidence in the vocation itself led the majority of religious orders to give only limited attention to teacher preparation.

With only a limited amount of time for the education of novices, congregations focused on character formation and general intellectual development; teacher training had a much lower priority. Of greatest importance to every congregation was to inspire in every novice a sense of community tradition and commitment to the rule of the founder of the order. This is not to

5. Ibid., p. 9.

say that teacher preparation was completely ignored.   Young
novices at the mother house were assigned to parishes with large
numbers of experienced sister-teachers who, in turn, trained the
novices to master the parochial classroom.   In the manner of a
craft, the "master teachers" trained their apprentices.[6]

This craft system was the predominant form of sister-teacher
preparation for many decades.   In fact, the craft system lasted
long after Catholic educators admitted that it was a poor method
of teacher training.   It remained popular for several reasons.
First, it was economical; it cost parish pastors little to have a
few novices working in their schools and often the choice was between a novice or no teacher at all.   Second, by assigning the
responsibility of teacher training to working sister-teachers,
superiors could devote almost all of the novices' time at the
mother house to the cultivation of the religious vocation and the
development of community spirit.   Third, the craft system allowed
the religious orders to get the nuns into the schools as quickly
as possible, thereby meeting the demand for sisters to staff increasing numbers of parish schools.   All of these factors contributed to the longevity of the craft system of sister-teacher preparation.[7]

It was clear to most Catholic educators that it would be
difficult to end the craft system as long as the demand for
sister-teachers remained high.   Yet no matter how many novices
were sent out each year, there were never enough vocations to

6. Ibid., p. 14.

7. Ibid., pp. 9-22.

meet the demand. Statistics compiled by Mary Oates on the occu-
pational distribution of sisters in the Archdiocese of Boston
show the impact of this demand.[8]

Boston nuns had always worked in a variety of occupations,
including hospital work, social welfare, and of course teaching.
But the demand for teachers forced increasing percentages of sisters into the classroom; by 1890, well over half of the sisters
in the archdiocese were working as teachers. As Oates points
out, "young women entering church service were encouraged to join
teaching communities in order to meet this need. These communities grew rapidly and were remarkably youthful."[9] The situation
in Boston was not unique; the youth and lack of experience of
sister-teachers across the country was the norm in most dioceses
in the nineteenth century.

The experiences of sister-teachers varied to some extent
from diocese to diocese, and even from decade to decade within a
single diocese, depending on the commitment of the bishops and
parish pastors to the establishment of parish schools. In some
eastern dioceses such as New York and Philadelphia, sister-
teachers received support from the Church establishment. But in
other dioceses, women religious were on their own. The following
portraits of four religious orders -- two each in Chicago and
Milwaukee -- document both experiences. In Chicago, religious
orders were left to fend for themselves and work directly with

8. Mary J. Oates, "Organized Volunteerism: The Catholic
Sisters of Massachusetts, 1870-1940," American Quarterly 30
(Winter 1978): 652-680.

9. Ibid., p. 656.

parish pastors in the staffing of specific schools. In Milwaukee, however, the bishops worked closely with the religious orders to insure that all of the schools in the diocese had the
necessary number of sister-teachers. Such portraits also provide
a glimpse of the arduous and uncertain life of the sister-teacher
in nineteenth-century America.

II

The history of women religious in Chicago in the nineteenth
century was, in the words of Edward Kantowicz, an "administrative
nightmare."[10] Dozens of congregations worked in the diocese,
some at the request of the bishop, others at the request of a
parish pastor. Each congregation was semi-autonomous, operating
independently within the diocese. They raised their own funds,
established their own schools, hospitals, and asylums when and
where they saw fit; and they closed these institutions when support declined. It is not surprising, therefore, that generalizations about the experiences of sister-teachers in Chicago are
hard to come by. The portraits that follow -- of the Sisters of
Mercy and the Sisters of Charity of the Blessed Virgin Mary --
offer a useful glimpse of the range of these experiences.

The Sisters of Mercy was the first Catholic religious order
to establish itself in Chicago. On September 23, 1846, five sisters arrived in the city at the invitation of Bishop William
Quarter. Led by Mother Mary Agatha O'Brien, a twenty-four-year-

10. Edward R. Kantowicz, <u>Corporation Sole: Cardinal Mundelein
and Chicago Catholicism</u> (Notre Dame, 1982), p. 85.

old Irish immigrant, the sisters quickly involved themselves in a variety of charitable activities that won them praise from city leaders.   Within a half a dozen years after their arrival, they would be responsible for the first parochial school, the first night school, the first orphan asylum, and the major hospital in the city.   Their commitment to the general improvement of urban life was evident in their every venture.[11]

Their first efforts were in education.   Less than a month after their arrival they opened two schools -- one for boys and a second for girls -- in the rear of their convent.   Both schools charged tuition and the funds were used for the support of the order.   Even with the fees, both institutions quickly reached their maximum enrollments of fifty students each.   The girls school was particularly popular and enrollment was increased to seventy students in 1849.   The Mercy sisters had a reputation for providing quality instruction, especially for girls.[12]

Yet the funds collected through tuition payments were not sufficient to cover even the modest expenses of the order in Chicago.   The Mercy sisters had come to the diocese at the invitation of a bishop who had promised to "provide amply" in support of the order.   But when the sisters arrived, Quarter was unable to make good on his promise.   Rather than abandon their new mission, O'Brien sought funds outside the diocese.   In a letter to the Association for the Propagation of the Faith in Lyon, France,

---

11. Mother Gabriel O'Brien, Reminiscences of Seventy Years (Chicago, 1916); M. Eulalia Herron, The Sisters of Mercy in the United States, (New York, 1929), pp. 49-59.

12. Herron, Sisters of Mercy, pp. 55-56.

she noted that Quarter could provide little support. She went on to explain that nuns "do not usually bring a dowry to the convent in this country and we are obliged to keep a pay school to enable us to live."[13] O'Brien asked for funds to buy land for an asylum and a free school and the Association responded with a gift of $4,000. The money was used to purchase twenty acres of prime, lake-front property. This legacy seemed to give the Mercy sisters a substantial measure of financial security and autonomy within the diocese.

Yet their security and autonomy was far more fragile than O'Brien realized. Quarter had purchased the land for the order with the intention of transfering legal title, but his untimely death in 1848 prevented him from completing the transaction. The temporary administrator of the diocese did fulfill the bishop's intention and the order received custody of the deed. But the new bishop, James O. Van de Velde, rejected this action and demanded that the order return the title to the diocese. O'Brien refused and threatened to withdraw the sisters from the diocese if the order's property rights were not guaranteed. After months of wrangling,the Mercy sisters won their case. The lake front property remained in the hands of the order as a corporation sanctioned by the Illinois general assembly.[14]

Its endowment secure for the time being, the order turned its attention to providing additional social services to both the

13. O'Brien to the Association for the Propagation of the Faith, December 4, 1847, copy in the AAC.

14. Kathleen Healy, Frances Warde (New York, 1973), pp. 204-205.

Catholic and the non-Catholic community of Chicago. The foremost
challenge accepted by the Mercy sisters was the operation of the
major hospital in the city. Founded as the Illinois General Hospital in February of 1851, it was renamed and reincorporated as
the "Mercy Hospital and Orphan Asylum of Chicago" in June of
1852. Assuming responsibility for the hospital made the Mercy
sisters the primary health care providers in this booming frontier community. Even with such an important obligation, the
order did not back away from their earlier commitment to education. The sisters established a free school on the north side of
the city in May of 1850, and opened a second academy for girls in
December of 1854.

In spite of these and other contributions to Catholicism in
Chicago, the relationship between the Mercy sisters and the diocesan leadership never quite recovered from the bitter contest
between O'Brien and Van de Velde. In fact, on several occasions
in the 1850s and 1860s, the order clashed with Van de Velde's
successors over the control of Mercy institutions. Rather than
submit to episcopal control, the order closed three parish
schools.

Yet on the control of their lake front property, the very
symbol of their independence, the Mercy sisters capitulated to
episcopal pressure. O'Brien died in an epidemic in 1854, and her
successor as superior did not have the resolve needed to fight
the bishop. Shortly after O'Brien's death, Bishop Anthony
O'Regan obtained the title to the disputed property. By the end

of the 1860s, the Sisters of Mercy had lost most of their autonomy within the diocese.[15]

Relations between the order and the diocese improved in the
last three decades of the century. Both Bishop Thomas Foley and
Mother Genevieve were determined to ease the tension that had
existed in the past. Tragedies such as the Great Fire of 1871
and the cholera epidemic of 1873 were situations that encouraged
the order to work with the bishop.

Yet it was the ever increasing demand for teachers that expanded the involvement of the Mercy sisters in Chicago Catholic
life. In fact, the demand was so great as to shift the order
away from their traditional involvement in health care and child
welfare into parochial education. The Mercy sisters staffed the
school of All Saints parish in 1875, handling an enrollment of
350 students. In 1881, they opened St. Gabriel's parish school,
followed by St. Patrick's school in South Chicago two years
later. In 1884, a new Mercy school was opened in St. James'
parish and a year later two more schools were added to the Mercy
list -- one in St. Rose of Lima parish and the other in St.
Elizabeth's parish. By 1896, the golden anniversary of the
Sisters of Mercy in Chicago, the order had 193 sisters and 23
novices teaching more than 5,000 pupils in Chicago's parochial
schools. It was a noteworthy achievement for an order with such a
troubled history in the diocese.[16]

---

15. Herron, Sisters of Mercy, pp. 59-63; Healy, Frances Warde,
pp. 205-206.

16. Herron, Sisters of Mercy, pp. 64-65.

The experiences of the Sisters of Charity of the Blessed Virgin Mary, better known as the BVM sisters, were very different from those of the Sisters of Mercy. In fact, the establishment of the BVM sisters in Chicago was the most important move in establishing the order outside of the narrow confines of the Archdiocese of Dubuque in Iowa.[17] The success of the Chicago congregation was self-evident in the order's operation of nearly forty parish schools and a variety of other educational institutions by the end of the century.

It all began with a simple invitation in 1867 from Arnold Damen, the Jesuit pastor of Holy Family parish. Previous efforts to attract the order to Chicago had failed because the Bishop of Dubuque, the order's spiritual sponsor, refused to allow the BVM sisters to expand outside his diocese. But by 1867, the order was of sufficient size to justify expansion and Chicago was seen as an ideal location for a new congregation.

Informal negotiations for the move to Chicago began as a conversation between Damen and Sister Margaret Mann. At the time Damen was giving a mission in Davenport, Iowa. "He wants our Sisters, six or nine to teach the Paracal [sic] school," she wrote to her superiors. "He would give them a house furnished and an oratory with Mass once or twice a week, two hundred and fifty Dollars each . . . . and the Fathers will have them under

---

17. M. Jane Coogan, The Price of Our Heritage: History of the Sisters of Charity, BVM, (2 vols., Dubuque, Iowa, 1975), 1:374.

their own protection, and in the Course of time if the Community wishes to buy the property, it will be all their own."[18]

Formal negotiations between Damen and T. J. Donaghue, the priest counselor of the order, got underway shortly thereafter. The terms outlined in Mann's letter were acceptable to the order, and when Damen arrived in Dubuque to give a Lenten mission in 1867, the agreement was formalized. The order was ecstatic. "Our sisters are called to fill a position which no order yet was intended for," wrote Father Philip Laurent, "and that is teaching our parochial schools and popularizing Catholicity among the masses . . . . I am confident that their being called to Chicago is the beginning of a new era for them."[19] Donaghue shared in this elation, but understood that new opportunities brought new challenges. "Chicago is ours, thank God," he wrote to Mann. "How and where to find teachers and all good ones."[20]

Seven sisters were assigned to Chicago in early August 1867. They were a motley collection in social background and they were led by the forty-four year old Mother Mary Agatha Hurley. For the most part they were young -- the oldest had been a sister for less than five years and the majority were still novices or only recently professed sisters. In fact, the novices had been put through an intense course in pedagogy that summer to prepare them for Chicago. It was the best that Donaghue could do under the circumstances. The sisters quickly settled themselves into their

18. Quoted in Coogan, Price of Our Heritage, 1:377.

19. Quoted in Ibid., 1:378-379.

20. Quoted in Ibid., 1:377.

convent and prepared to open their school in an abandoned warehouse about seven blocks away.

The arrival of the BVM sisters was an important event in the parish and both the sisters and the students were nervous in anticipation. "Their first problem was to find the school in which they were to teach," wrote the historian of the order. "In this they had little trouble, for as they approached the general area they were alerted to its location by a bedlam of high-pitched feminine voices, and soon came into sight of a milling crowd of hundreds of girls of all ages, pushing, shoving, chasing each other about, jumping over gates and climbing over fences . . . . Of necessity, the sisters would learn the arts of regimentation and command."[21] Indeed they did, for the sisters were forced to deal with large numbers in every class. By September 2, nine BVM sisters were teaching in two schools with a combined enrollment of 500 students.

The sisters were popular in large part because they followed Damen's advice to emphasize basic secular instruction as well as religious development. "The children, like their parents, belong to him," wrote one of the sisters referring to Damen, "so we follow his ideas in all our rooms."[22] As a result, the number of students kept rising. "The Sisters have now about seven hundred children," wrote Damen on September 12, "and if we had room, I think that after awhile, they would have a thousand."[23] Six

21. Ibid., 1:381.

22. Ibid.

23. Quoted in Ibid., 1:381.

weeks later the number of sisters had increased to eleven and enrollment was over 850 in the two schools. "God be praised," concluded Donaghue in a report written on October 22. "The Sisters are full of their mission."[24] It was an extraordinary beginning for any religious congregation.

Yet there was hardship in such rapid expansion. Long hours and hard work undermined the health of the sisters. During the first years of the BVM sisters in Chicago, several sisters experienced severe bouts of illness, and Hurley herself was chronically ill. She repeatedly requested relief from her duties as superior, believing that her constant illness was a handicap to the success of the mission.

Donaghue refused to replace her. "You say that the doctor speaks plainly and the Jesuit Father advises resignation," responded Donaghue to one such request. "Well bless God for your own Father T. J. D. gives you hope."[25] Later petitions also were rebuffed. "No, I wish you to remain in Chicago," he wrote, "when I go to Heaven, if there is health for you, I will obtain it."[26] Hurley stayed on in Chicago as Donaghue had requested, but lived in constant pain for the next thirty-four years. Other sisters had nervous breakdowns; still others died in a small pox epidemic in 1883.

Yet the expansion of the parochial school system in Chicago in the 1870s and 1880s was possible in part because of the wil-

---

24. Quoted in Ibid., 1:385.

25. Quoted in Ibid., 1:410.

26. Ibid.

lingness of the BVM sisters to transcend their hardship and take on institutions outside Damen's Holy Family Parish. As the Irish moved out of Holy Family and built new parishes in other parts of the city, they encouraged their pastors to call on the BVM sisters.

The BVM sisters also staffed the schools in parishes that were carved out of Holy Family parish. In 1871, for example, the order moved into Annunciation parish on the northwest side of the city and enrolled over 800 students. Three years later, they moved into St. Pius parish on the southside. In 1876, they added St. Bridget's in Bridgeport to their rolls, and two years after that, Holy Angels school on the near west side. In 1882, Sacred Heart parish opened a school with BVM sisters in the classroom and the following year, St. Vincent de Paul parish on the northside of the city called for the sisters. As the Third Plenary Council mandated the establishment of parish schools, the demand for BVM sisters increased. Eventually, they would staff nearly forty parish schools in the archdiocese.[27]

In 1884, Mother Mary Clarke, the founder of the BVM order, committed to paper her philosophy for the operation of the order's schools. "Let us be convinced from the beginning," she wrote, "that we can never attract our pupils to us and cause them to take pleasure in acquiring a knowledge of our Holy Religion unless we can justly merit their confidence and that of their parents in our ability as efficient teachers; if both one and the other find not in our schools what they could find in others.

27. Ibid.

Let us then acquire and impart secular knowledge with a view to this and with a holy intelligent zeal, keep our schools progressive with the times in which we live; by inventiveness and forethought, utilize our knowledge and our time to advance our pupils judiciously and thus secure for our schools a good name, which will be the bait to draw young and innocent souls from the schools of infidelity and immorality."[28]   In these few sentences, Clarke captured the shrewd, practical philosophy that was the foundation for the success of the BVM sisters in Chicago.

The Sisters of Mercy and the Sisters of Charity of the Blessed Virgin Mary experienced complimentary, but distinct histories in the nation's second city.   The Mercy sisters' position as the first religious order in the diocese did them little good. In fact, the order suffered during the first twenty-five years of diocesan affairs due to the instability of the hierarchy.   It was not until the 1870s, when the diocese had achieved a significant measure of peace, that the Mercy sisters began to prosper.   In contrast to this turbulent history, the BVM sisters benefited enormously from the sponsorship of Arnold Damen and the Jesuits of Holy Family parish.   More importantly, the order started small in Chicago -- a few schools in a single parish -- and moved into new parishes gradually.   This cautious expansion, plus the common sense of Donaghue and Clarke, allowed the BVM sisters to avoid some of the growing pains that plagued the Sisters of Mercy.

---

28. Quoted in Ibid., 2:209.

III

The experiences of sister-teachers in Milwaukee were both similar and different from those of their colleagues in Chicago. There were some very obvious differences, of course. Milwaukee nuns, for example, did not suffer the level of hardship experienced by the Sisters of Mercy in Chicago and all of the women religious in Milwaukee benefited from the stable leadership of bishops Henni and Heiss. This is not to say that religious life in Milwaukee was without trial and tribulation. Indeed, there were hardships. Yet the bishops placed a high priority on maintaining a stable work force in their schools. To do so, they worked closely with the superiors of several religious orders to insure a steady supply of sister-teachers. The religious orders were attracted to Milwaukee because the diocese had a reputation for stability and commitment.

The experiences of the Daughters of Charity in Milwaukee were similar to some extent to those of the Sisters of Mercy in Chicago, at least superficially. The Charity sisters were the first religious order in the diocese and among the first to establish social institutions.[29] On August 31, 1846, the Charity sisters established the first parochial school in Milwaukee in the basement of St. Peter's Church, and from that point on, the order continued to serve the city center until the turn of the century.

---

29. Peter L. Johnson, The Daughters of Charity in Milwaukee, 1846-1946, (Milwaukee, 1946).

This early school was very primitive. "The school desks were wide, box-like affairs," noted the historian of the order, "and made of common boards. Not being expected . . . to write, smaller tots were not given desks, but were seated on benches along the wall."[30] Late in 1846, the sisters moved to a new convent, a two-story building on Van Buren Street. The school remained in the basement of St. Peter's Church.

Like the Mercy sisters in Chicago, the Daughters of Charity arrived in Milwaukee without any endowment. To raise money for their free parochial school, the Charity sisters opened St. Joseph Female Academy in one of the wings of their convent. Tuition for the school ranged up to four dollars per quarter, depending on the level of instruction. Even though the school was a source of income, it was not enough to support the order. More sisters were needed so that the enrollment could be increased. "There is an excellent spirit among us," Henni wrote to the superior of the order, "even among the Protestants, and hardly a day passes when Protestant parents do not bring their daughters to the academy, the colors of which you perceive are already hoisted. Mother, you do not wish us to have them taken down."[31] Mother Etienne Hall agreed and a third sister was sent to Milwaukee to work in the school.

The Catholic community continued to increase and the demand for parochial education required that the sisters move their free

---

30. Ibid., p. 17.

31. Mother Etienne Hall, 1845-1855 (Emmitsburg, Md, 1939), pp. 15-16.

school from the basement of St. Peter's Church to a four-room
house. The move took place in 1849, but by 1853 increased space
requirements required the sisters to switch the free school and
the academy. A third move took place in 1874 when the school was
moved to the recently completed bishop's hall.

As successful as the Charity sisters were in the early years
of the diocese, the order never much expanded beyond the confines
of the cathedral parish. In a diocese overwhelming dominated by
German Catholics, the English-speaking Daughters of Charity con-
fined their ministry to the small Irish community in Milwaukee.[32]

Of all the many responsibilities faced by Bishop Henni
during his first years in Milwaukee, none was more important to
him than the recruitment of religious orders. Without teaching
sisters, there would be only a handful of Catholic schools. He
was pleased with the arrival of the Daughters of Charity in 1846,
but hardly satisfied. In a diocese dominated by Germans, he knew
that he would need large numbers of German nuns.

Henni was very successful in attracting German sisters because of his contacts with the Ludwig Mission Society in Bavaria
and the Leopoldine Association of Vienna. He often was the first
to learn of the imminent arrival of new sisters from Europe. "To
my great joy," he wrote in 1846, "I was told in Baltimore that
the School Sisters of Bavaria are expected. I hope I may get
some of them for the benefit of our young German people. There

---

32. Johnson, Daughters of Charity, pp. 13-26.

is no doubt that not a few would join them from the west and thus enlarge their community."[33]

But Henni's wish was not fulfilled quickly and he became anxious. "How is it that you have nothing to say," he wrote to his friend, Father Joseph Mueller in Bavaria, "whether the School Sisters really intend to come to Milwaukee. I am anxious to know whether this, my wish, could be fulfilled before the year is over."[34] The School Sisters of Notre Dame finally came to Milwaukee in 1851 after Henni raised the money needed for their support.

In their first year in the diocese, the four Notre Dame sisters, led by Mother Caroline Freiss, devoted themselves to the basics. In January of 1851, they opened St. Mary's parochial school and were swamped with 130 students. As important as this school was, it did not generate the income needed to support the order. The German mission societies had promised aid, but the funds were not immediately available. To raise money, Freiss opened a music school, and later in 1851 a select academy for girls. The funds generated by these schools allowed Freiss to bring three more sisters to Milwaukee in April. By the end of 1851, the staff of eight was supporting two schools and a music academy.[35]

---

33. Henni to Joseph Mueller, August 7, 1846, ASFS, printed in Salesianum 37 (1942).

34. Henni to Mueller, January 24, 1848, ASFS, printed in Salesianum 38 (1943).

35. Mother Caroline and the School Sisters of Notre Dame in North America, (2 vols., St. Louis, 1928), 1:53-65.

Their second year in Milwaukee was no less active for the Notre Dame sisters. Their foremost project was the construction of a motherhouse. This structure would serve as the center of operations for the order for the next several decades.

In addition to opening the motherhouse, a structure that would take a decade to complete, the order also opened more schools. Freiss added a school at Mount Carmel, about eighty miles north of Milwaukee, and sent sisters to join the Redemptorists in Detroit to take charge of St. Mary's school in that city. In September, Notre Dame sisters opened Holy Trinity parochial school in West Milwaukee, a school attended by eighty boys and girls.

When she looked back on 1852, Freiss felt blessed. "Reports from many cities indicated that bishops and priests were learning to know the sisters and their work, especially from the children of the parishes, and the requests to obtain teachers for their parish schools were numerous . . . . Material blessings had also multiplied. Financial conditions had so improved that in nearly all the schools each teacher received a small salary."[36]

Yet the life of the Notre Dame sisters was not one of ease. The challenges and hardships they faced in maintaining a spiritual rule and in teaching children of all backgrounds were considerable. One report of the order written in 1856 gives evidence of the problems the sisters faced. "Each sister's development must be many-sided," wrote Anthony Urbanek, a spiritual counselor to the Milwaukee congregation, "as her activities are

---

36. Ibid., 1:69.

many and diverse. They receive in their schools the children of the wealthy, the refined, the educated; the children of the middle-classes of honest, God-fearing parentage, who form the bulk of our citizens; thirdly the children of the poorest in mental and material endowments. The sisters must be equally at home with all classes, she must adapt herself to all possible requirements; in a word, she must be trained to become all to all to win all to God."[37]

Urbanek went on to bemoan the difficulties of the task in a country in which Catholic children "are surrounded on all sides by examples of glaring atheism."[38] This was the challenge of the sister-teacher in Milwaukee. "A School Sister must cope with all this," concluded Urbanek, "and with her full power make reparation to God for all the insults heaped upon Him by those of her surroundings."[39]

In her annual report to the Ludwig Mission Society, submitted shortly before Urbanek's 1856 report, Freiss wrote of both her wealth and her poverty. "Thousands of children are waiting, in need of a Catholic school," she wrote. "To supply their needs a much greater number of sisters would be required. Even if we had them it would be impossible to shelter them in a Mother House which in spite of the new annex, is again too small for our numbers. Far less are we able to buy dwellings for our sisters

---

37. Urbanek to the Reverend R. Overkamp of the Ludwig Mission Society, May 6, 1856, quoted in Ibid., 1:105.

38. Ibid., 1:106.

39. Ibid.

on the missions where poverty presses in every way. Were it not for the grace of vocation, these young women could not endure their privations. After entering, they find every where poverty and self denial . . . . Conditions everywhere are favorable for the furthering of our work in the schools except that poverty hampers us at every step, especially in the erection of necessary buildings."[40] Freiss pleaded for funds to lighten the burden that she and the sisters faced.

Freiss herself was relieved of some of the administrative burden of directing her growing order. In August of 1856, Sister M. Theophilia assumed responsibilities as the mistress of candidates and superintendent of Milwaukee's parish schools. Relieved of these responsibilities, Freiss spent more time traveling between the order's three motherhouses in Milwaukee, New Orleans, and Baltimore.

The arduous nature of their work led Mother Caroline to request a change in the order's rule in the United States. Up until the late 1850s, the School Sisters of Notre Dame were required to say daily prayers, rising at midnight and again at four in the morning. This responsibility, in addition to a full day of teaching, taxed the average sister and contributed to frequent illness. In May of 1859, Pope Pius IX granted the order a dispensation from the specified prayers and substituted a less arduous regimen. The late 1850s also saw the order expand into new states. In 1859, schools were staffed in Missouri, Illinois, and

---

40. Freiss to the Ludwig Mission Society, May 1856, quoted in Ibid., 1:109.

Pennsylvania and a year later the order began work in dioceses in New Jersey and Iowa.[41]

In all of her work, Freiss continued to confide in and depend upon the counsel and contributions of the Ludwig Mission Society. Her annual letters of 1858 and 1862 reveal the continuing challenges faced by the order in the preparation of novices for the parochial school classroom. "To maintain her own position," she noted, "a School Sister must frequently use her influence indirectly only and must do so on account of the attitudes of the parents who resent more a fancied invasion of their authority, than from any cause presented by the children themselves."[42]

But classroom problems were surmountable. "All must be accomplished through love and patience," she added. But the very real poverty of the country limited the number of schools that could be sustained by the order. "The greater number remains poor," she added, "and if there are some who amass wealth, how many years are required to do so? Imagine a parish composed of the poorer or the middle classes. What a heavy burden for the individual are the running expenses!"[43] Freiss pleaded for more funds from her benefactors.

Perhaps she was thinking of the Poles who were arriving in Milwaukee in the 1860s. The School Sisters established the first

41. Ibid., 1:109-121.

42. Freiss to the Ludwig Mission Society, April 1858, quoted in Ibid., 1:122.

43. Freiss to the Ludwig Mission Society, April 1862, quoted in Ibid., 1:160.

Polish Catholic school in Milwaukee in 1869 and to staff it,
Freiss took a novel approach. Instead of sending German sisters
into the Polish school, she chose Irish novices. Her thinking
was clear. "In the nineteen years she had spent as the superior
of the congregation, she had received many sisters of Irish
ancestry, whose forebearers, like the Poles, had borne persecu-
tion for the Faith. Since Ireland and Poland were twin sisters
in suffering, why not let the Irish sisters, as they were sometimes called, come to the assistance of their companions."[44]
These first sister-teachers were quickly replaced by Polish
novices to the order who took great pride in teaching catechism
in their native tongue. In this process, Freiss avoided the natural antagonism that existed between the Germans and the Poles.

December of 1870 marked the twentieth anniversary of the
School Sisters of Notre Dame in Milwaukee. By that date the order had established 126 schools in seventeen dioceses in fourteen
states. All but six of these institutions were parochial elementary schools, and the vast majority of the parishes were German
Catholic. Along with the Franciscans, the School Sisters of
Notre Dame monopolized the German Catholic schools, not only in
Milwaukee, but also across the country. The order had come a
long way since arriving in Milwaukee twenty years earlier.

But not everyone was happy. In 1870, a group of citizens
from Port Washington, Wisconsin, complained to the state school
superintendent that the local school board was staffing the public schools with Notre Dame sisters, and that all children in

---

44. Ibid., 1:203.

these schools were being taught the Catholic religion. The
superintendent investigated these charges and as a result, the
public school staffed by the sisters was transformed into a parochial school. The plaintiffs could go no further with the case
because they could not find a lawyer willing to take the case to
court."[45]

A second case did reach the courts, however. Attacks on the
Notre Dame sisters in the May 1, 1873, issue of The Christian
Statesman were challenged in the Milwaukee courts by a coalition
of local Catholics. The case dragged on in the courts for more
than two years and served as a referendum on the work of the sisters. Finally, the editor of the Statesman agreed to apologize
for making slanderous remarks, but the retraction never received
the attention given to the original charges. The incident dam-
pened the celebration of the order's twenty-fifth anniversary in
Milwaukee.[46]

During the 1870s the sisters continued to face the same
problems that had plagued the order for the previous two decades.
To be sure, the order continued to expand, but not at a rate that
pleased Freiss. From the beginning of 1873 to the end of 1879,
for example, the order had offers to open seventy-six schools,
but could handle only forty-eight. The death of the first generation of sister-teachers had cut into expansion plans. "If those
zealous pastors could obtain sisters of other orders it would not
be so hard," she wrote, "but to think of the hundreds who must

---

45. Ibid., 1:209-210.

46. Ibid., 1:233-236.

grow up without the advantage of a Catholic education is heart rending."[47] This was the dilemma faced by the School Sisters of Notre Dame for the rest of the nineteenth century and even into the twentieth century.

In spite of these problems, the Notre Dame sisters thrived during the nineteenth century. As the home of a Notre Dame motherhouse, Milwaukee benefited enormously from the success of the order. Most important to bishops Henni and Heiss and their successors was the close proximity to a steady supply of sister-teachers for the German and Polish Catholic schools of the diocese. Because of the close working relationship between the leaders of the diocese and the order, Milwaukee's Catholic schools were rarely short of teachers.

IV

The leadership played by women religious in Catholic parochial education is obvious. In fact, in relative terms, it would not be difficult to make the case that teachers were the leaders in Catholic parochial education in the nineteenth century. "If adequate means could be found to measure the relative importance of personal influences," notes Mary Ewens, "it might well be shown that sisters' efforts were far more effective than those of bishops or priests."[48]

---

47. Ibid., 1:236.

48. Mary Ewens, "The Leadership of Nuns in Immigrant Catholicism," in Women and Religion in America, edited by Rosemary R. Ruether and Rosemary S. Keller, (New York, 1981), 1:101.

As Ewens and others have shown, the responsibilities of sister-teachers for the spiritual life of the American Church were extraordinary. They taught successive generations the basic tenets of the Faith "and gave them a solid grounding in Christian living and a sense of responsibility for the maintenance of a Christian atmosphere in the homes they would one day run and the religious instruction of their children."[49] One should attribute the expansion of the Catholic population not only to immigration, but also to the skills of sister-teachers in cultivating a life-long faith in generation after generation of American-born Catholics.

Overall, the experiences of women religious were extra-ordinary, not only in the specific context of American Catholicism, but also in the general context of American society. "In many aspects of their lives," notes Ewens, "nuns in nineteenth century America enjoyed opportunities open to few women of their time; involvement in meaningful work, access to administrative positions, freedom from the responsibilities of marriage and motherhood, opportunities to live in sisterhood, and egalitarian friendship. Perhaps it was this freedom from the restrictive roles usually ascribed to women that enabled them to exert such a powerful influence on the American Church."[50]

One also can see this achievement in the sheer size of the workforce. By the end of the nineteenth century there were more than 40,000 sisters working in dioceses in the United States --

---

49. Ibid., 1:101-102.

50. Ibid., 1:107.

four times the number of priests. The impact of the work of these women is difficult to overestimate.

Why, then, have women religious in general and sister-teachers in particular been ignored? These four vignettes provide only a glimpse into the experiences of sister-teachers in the nineteenth century. Indeed, the serious historical exploration of these extraordinary women has yet to be written.

The reason for this historiographical neglect is multi-faceted. Certainly the prejudices of earlier generations of Catholic historians led them to concentrate almost exclusively on the hierarchy. As a result, the history of priests, parishes, and women religious were almost completely ignored. It is also true that religious orders themselves were reluctant to have their stories told. Only recently have most religious orders of women organized their archives and made historical materials available for research. Whatever the cause, it is clear that historians of Catholicism can no longer ignore the extraordinary contributions of women religious to the life of the American Church, particularly in the establishment and operation of vital social institutions such as parochial schools.

CHAPTER VII

CATHOLIC SCHOOLBOOKS AND AMERICAN VALUES

The most controversial aspect of nineteenth century Catholic education was content. Just what was being taught in those parish classrooms and how did this instruction differ from public education? Many Americans were curious. Nativists argued that parochial schools indoctrinated children so that they could be manipulated by unscrupulous priests. They accused the parochial schools of being fundamentally un-American. Catholic schoolmen countered by proclaiming that parochial education was one of the highest acts of patriotism because it taught children to cherish national principles such as respect for home and family, reverence for God, and love of country. It was a public debate long on rhetoric and bombast and short on facts and figures. Neither side could get beyond polemics.

There is no question that parochial school students had a distinctive classroom experience, one different from the public schools. Catholic schools were staffed by women whose very dress proclaimed their religious heritage. Religious pictures and statues were prominently displayed in the classrooms and daily instruction was interlaced with Catholic and religious examples. Many Catholic schools -- German and Polish in particular -- also incorporated native languages and culture into the curriculum. It was not quite the same experience as public schooling.

Beyond these important but external differences, however, there were a number of similarities between the two types of schooling. These similarities are most evident in a comparison of the content of the schoolbooks used in public and parochial institutions. Even though these do not provide evidence of the total classroom experience, such books do indicate many of the values that were highly regarded by public and parochial school-men. Such textbooks were also important because they made an impression on the students if only by the fact that many passages were committed to memory.

Before comparing public and parochial schoolbooks, a word is needed about the adoption of Catholic textbooks from one diocese to the next. Unlike many aspects of Catholic education in the nineteenth century, Catholic schoolbooks did not differ much from one diocese to the next. Only a few publishers -- D. & J. Sadlier and Benziger Brothers most notably -- ventured into Catholic textbook publishing in the nineteenth century. All of these books were very similar in content and were used in many parishes in most dioceses. Thus Catholic students in Chicago and Milwaukee very likely were reading the same lessons as their counterparts in Boston and New York. But were these Catholic students learning the same values as their neighbors in the public schools? A careful examination of the two types of textbooks brings to light few substantive differences.[1]

---

1. See especially Andrew M. Greeley and Peter H. Rossi, The Education of Catholic Americans (Chicago, 1966), which recorded the findings of a 1963 study of Catholic education conducted by the National Opinion Research Center of the University of Chicago. Also see Peter H. Rossi and Alice S. Rossi, "Some Ef-

Because scholars have studied public schoolbooks in great detail, it will be necessary only to summarize the prevailing historical assessment.[2] The hundreds of schoolbooks published in the nineteenth century emphasized the same values -- patriotism, piety, deference, thrift, honesty, and diligence.[3] Most frequently, these schoolbooks stressed the educational value of nature. "By analogy, nature was used in numerous stories for moral instruction. The industry of the ant and the bee and the fecklessness of the grasshopper were ever present in the pages of nineteenth century schoolbooks."[4] Although their analogies were sometimes vague, public schoolbook authors throughout the nineteenth century consistently portrayed nature as the provider, protector, and teacher.

Patriotism and superiority of the United States was the second theme. In fact, textbook writers depicted the United States in almost theological terms, as if it were a nation of God's chosen people. American citizenship, according to public schoolbooks, was based on reliance, love of liberty, and democratic feelings. These qualities were found in men like Benjamin

fects of Parochial School Education in America," _Daedelus_, 90 (Spring, 1961): 300-328. Both of these studies show that Catholic education did not have an isolating affect on Catholic children; neither was there a negative impact on the economic achievement of these children nor a negative impact on their social attitudes.

2. Ruth Miller Elson, _Guardians of Tradition_ (Lincoln, 1964); Richard D. Mosier, _Making the American Mind: Social and Moral Ideas in McGuffey Readers_ (New York, 1965); Charles Carpenter, _History of American Schoolbooks_ (Philadelphia, 1963); John A. Neitz, _Our Textbooks_ (Pittsburgh, 1961).

3. Elson, _Guardians_, pp. 338, 340-341.

4. _Ibid._, p. 19.

Franklin, George Washington, and Abraham Lincoln, all frequent textbook heroes. "As the modern chosen people," notes historian Ruth Miller Elson, "Americans had a special motive for piety, and concomitantly, they had a special motive for patriotism; love of the American nation was a correlative of love of God."[5]

The third theme expressed by public schoolbook authors was a conservative code of social behavior. The social virtues most frequently praised were economic -- industry and frugality for example. Conversely, undesirable traits such as idleness were stigmatized as sinful.[6] The American dream was attainable by all, and wealth was the result of applying the virtues of diligence, temperance, honesty, and compliance. Schoolbook authors reminded their young readers that true quality lived in virtue rather than rank and warned the lower classes against disillusionment or discontent. America was a nation run by the meritorious rather than by the well-born. Ultimately, public schoolmen stressed that middle-class independence and moderate comfort rather than opulence were the most desirable goals.

The message of the public school text was clear and conservative. Authors repeatedly returned to these themes to encourage docility, diligence, and patriotism in children. Such writers taught their readers to accept the status quo and to learn to achieve within its boundaries. There was no malevolence in this instruction. Educators -- writers and teachers alike -- believed that a large part of their duty was to help their students to

---

5. Ibid., pp. 62, 192.

6. Ibid., pp. 251-252, 256-257, 267, 277.

adapt to the rigors of an industrialized society. The values implicit in public schoolbooks were recognized to contribute to
material and social success and therefore highly valued by most
Americans.

The implicit themes of nineteenth century Catholic schoolbooks were very similar to those in public texts. The nature of
that similarity, however, requires close attention. The publication of Catholic educational materials in the United States is
almost as old as the nation itself. In 1785, Robert Molyneaux, a
Philadelphia priest, published A Spelling Primer for Children
with a Catholic Catechism Annexed. The following year The Roman
Catholic Primer was released by an unknown publisher in
Philadelphia, making that city the center of small Catholic publishing industry. Mathew Carey continued this tradition with two
works published at the turn of the century: The Child's Guide to
Spelling and Reading and The American Primer. Yet it is important to note that the early Catholic publishing trade was a
localized affair. It was not until the 1840s when the industry
spread to Baltimore, New York, and Boston, that the use of Catholic texts became common.[7]

The first Catholic publishing houses commonly modified European texts for American audiences. One of the nineteenth century's most popular series was that written by the Christian
Brothers of Ireland. First published in the United States in
1843 by Eugene Cuminsky, the books were very popular in cities

---

7. James A. Burns, The Growth and Development of the Catholic
School System in the United States (New York, 1912), pp. 136-145.

with large Irish populations. Perhaps the most popular of the early editions was published by Joseph Dunigan of New York in 1852. The stories selected by the publisher closely paralleled those in public texts.

The Dunigan edition of the Christian Brother's Second Book of Reading Lessons, for example, emphasized two of the three public school themes: the educational value of nature and the value of a conservative code of behavior.[8]   The Christian Brothers stated the first theme more explicitly than many of the public school authors. One key passage in the text emphasized that nature was the manifestation of the law of God. Through nature, God taught his children how to live. Thus, the Christian Brothers encouraged school children to look to nature to learn the will of God. The book also presented nature as an educator. The bees, for example, were admired for their "wisdom and government, their prudent habits, and their instructive example."[9]

The second theme in Catholic texts -- conservative social values -- also resembled that presented in public texts. Each lesson concluded with a moral. "Shall I tell what my father said when he was telling us of a thief who passed by our house with his hands tied on his way to prison?" asked one character. "He said that those who begin with small offenses, finish with great ones."[10]   In another story, Frank, a "thoughtless boy," ventured

---

8. Brothers of the Christian Schools, The Second Book of Reading Lessons (New York, 1852), pp. 9, 54.

9. Ibid., p. 65.

10. Ibid., p. 11.

onto thin ice after being warned against it. He fell through, of
course, and as he stood dripping wet, Frank's father reminded him
that "those who do not attend to good advice will suffer for
it."[11]

Thirty years later the Christian Brothers continued to emphasize these same themes and their texts were still popular.
Nature was still used to explain the glory of God, and animals
and plants were still anthropomorized to explain various human
qualities -- intelligence and bravery, for example.

There was, however, an increasing sophistication in the
stories about nature. Even the Elementary Reader in the Christian Brothers New Series of 1882 explained mankind's relationship
to nature in a direct manner. In a story about the use of
plants, the Brothers wrote of the great value of trees. "Every
bit of wood that you see once grew as a tree," reminded the
author. "What should we do without wood? The roofs of our
houses are made of it and so are the floors and doors and window
frames. Our tables and chairs and chests of drawers are all of
wood and we have wooden boxes, wooden casts, and wooden
fences . . . . God made all these things and they teach us how
wise and good he is."[12] This bluntness was characteristic of
most of the stories about nature in the Elementary Reader.

Such language, however, was not characteristic of the
stories focusing on social values. Lessons entitled "Choice of

---

11. Ibid., pp. 22, 46; italics in text.

12. Brothers of the Christian Schools, Elementary Reader (West
Chester, NY, 1883), p. 75.

Trades," "The Truant," and "The Orphan," were written in verse
and in language reminiscent of the 1852 edition. The first story
spoke of the satisfaction of farming, carpentry, blacksmithing,
masonry, shoemaking, and printing, and concluded with the following doggerel: "Whatever we do this thing we'll say, /We'll do
our work in the very best way. /And you shall see, if you know
us then, /We'll be good and honest and useful men."[13] The second
story noted the foolishness of running away from home; the main
character was without food, shelter, or medical care all because
he left his "good and kind" parents. In the final stanza the
truant begs for help from an unidentified woman: "If you should
have a child distress'd, /My grief with pity see; /With such a
friend may he be bless'd, /As you shall pity me."[14] The reader
was also asked to pity "The Orphan" for whom the only hope was
faith in God.[15] The message of all three stories was clear despite the poor quality of the verse. The emphasis on diligent,
honest work habits and devotion to parents resembled the themes
expressed in public school texts.

The popularity of the Christian Brothers' books did not go
unchallenged. In New York City, D. & J. Sadlier began publishing a series of texts in the 1840s and the books grew in popularity throughout the nineteenth century.[16] By the mid-1870s, the
Sadlier books were so popular that they offered two different

---

13. Ibid., pp. 37-40.

14. Ibid., pp. 133-135.

15. Ibid., pp. 170-171.

16. Burns, Growth and Development, p. 143.

series of readers. The most popular was the "Excelsior Series" which included six readers, a history text, and a geography text. The style and content of the "Excelsior" readers were very similar to that of both its Catholic and public competitors and the themes were almost identical. Like the Christian Brothers texts, the Sadlier books stressed the educational value of nature and the importance of a conservative code of behavior.

The themes in the Excelsior Third Reader were presented allegorically, as in the public texts. This was particularly true of stories about nature or natural settings. The growth of an oak tree from an acorn emphasized the value of patience. A father told his son that a boy's life resembled that of a young tree. "Prisons and Penitentiaries are like the ropes and chains upon crooked trees which were not guided correctly." A passing bee taught the value of work to an idle young boy; the author concluded: "I know not if the idler caught, /This lesson from the busy bee, /But through his mind there came a thought, /As it flew by him: 'Is there naught, /No work to do for me?'"[17]

Parables and stories also taught social values. Young Vincent accidently trampled his father's favorite plant and admitted it with trepidation. But Vincent's father was not angry. "Though I regret the loss of the plant which has cost me so much to preserve," he said, "it has been the means of proving to me that I have a son in whose words I can place confidence."[18]

---

17. Sadlier's Excelsior Third Reader (New York, 1878), p. 44-45.

18. Ibid., pp. 116-117.

Another story spoke of ambition and reminded the students that "the desire to excell is good as long as the desire of God's approbation is strongest in your mind."[19] A third story emphasized that "if God puts you in a place where you must live by the work of your hands, you may be sure that it is the very thing that is good for you."[20] Implicit in all the stories was the message that proper values were their own reward.

The stories in the Excelsior Fourth Reader were similar in spirit to those on the Excelsior Third Reader but the emphasis on proper social values was even more pronounced. This is not to say that there are no stories about the educational value of nature. In fact, the book included the famous tale about the grasshopper who fiddled away his summer only to starve in the winter. Lessons often focused on the loyalty of dogs and the freedom of birds.

The Fourth Reader, however, stressed social behavior. This volume encouraged the emulation of historical figures such as George Washington and Benjamin Franklin. Even more to the point, the book spoke of "useful" people. "There are many ways of being useful," began one lesson. "You are useful -- you who from a love of order and a wish to see everyone happy, watch carefully that nothing should be out of place, that nothing should be injured, that everything should shine with cleanliness. You are useful -- you who are prevented by others from working because they doubt your capacity, you who get snubbed and have employ-

---

19. Ibid., p. 159.

20. Ibid., pp. 40-43.

ments given to you that are quite unfitted to your ability, and yet who keep silence and are humble and good natured."[21]   The Excelsior Fourth Reader noted that justice came in heaven rather than on this earth.

In 1874, the publishing firm of Benziger Brothers entered the competition by introducing the "Catholic National Series of Readers." Because the author of the series was Richard Gilmour, the conservative bishop of Cleveland, the books were particularly appealing to traditional parishes. Yet there were few differences between the Benziger series and its competitors. The familiar themes about nature and social values were repeated. The "Catholic National Series" New First Reader included a lesson about the idle child who learns to work from animals.[22]   Another story spoke of love and obedience when a young girl, asked by her mother what she had learned in school, replied: "I learned that I must be a good child and love God. I must love my parents too and do what they tell me."[23]   The First Reader served as a preface to more explicit presentations of the educational value of nature and the importance of "proper" behavior.

The Second Reader and the Third Reader sharpened the focus on nature and social values. In a story about the gifts of the sun, the Sun speaks: "I warm the earth to life. I make the shrubs and trees grow and cover them with flowers and fruit. I

21. Sadlier's Excelsior Fourth Reader (New York, 1878), pp. 100-101.

22. Richard Gilmour, First Reader, "Catholic National Series," (New York, 1877), pp. 81-83.

23. Ibid., p. 24.

draw up the clouds and send down rain to fill your springs and rivers."[24] A second story noted that "the cow is not as handsome as the horse but it is nonetheless useful."[25]

The clearest lesson about the educational value of nature came in the Third Reader. The story entitled "What the Earth Produces for Man," added an important qualification to nature's gifts. "Providence has given few things ready for the use of man," wrote Bishop Gilmour. "It seems to have been the will of God that man should exist and improve his reason and other powers, by fitting for his own use, the products of the earth."[26]

Proper social behavior was an important topic in the Second Reader. "Work while you work," began one poem. "Play while you play /That is the way to be cheerful and gay /Moments are useless /When trifled away /So work while you work /And play while you play."[27] And, as always, parental love and respect were a crucial part of social values. "We must honor our parents," wrote Gilmour, "and do their will in all that is not sin. A child that loves his parents will do all he can to please them."[28] Even though "The Catholic National Series" was supposed to be conservative because its author was a leading conservative, in fact the

---

24. Richard Gilmour, Second Reader, "Catholic National Series," (New York, 1877), pp. 26-27.

25. Ibid., p. 17.

26. Richard Gilmour, Third Reader, "Catholic National Series," (New York, 1877), pp. 42-43.

27. Gilmour, Second Reader, p. 16.

28. Ibid., pp. 34-35.

content of the series differed very little from any of the
others.

The overwhelming majority of Catholic schoolbooks were in
complete thematic agreement with their public school counterparts. Yet it would be erroneous to think of the two types of
books as one and the same. On one point in particular, parochial
schoolbooks differed: the Catholic perspective on the American
past was clearly partisan. Catholic schoolmen, to be sure,
agreed that America was superior to other nations. Yet they also
felt compelled to emphasize the continuing involvement and contributions of Catholics to the American experience. Lesson after
lesson recalled the exploits of American Catholic heroes from the
obvious such as Commodore John Barry and Bishop John Carroll to
the preposterous such as "Bishop Gorda," a missionary in Green-
land.

Parochial schoolmen hoped that such instruction would encourage Catholic children to become involved in American affairs.
"We desire that the history of the United States should be taught
in all our Catholic schools," noted one schoolman. "We must keep
firm and solid the liberties of our country by keeping fresh and
noble memories of the past and thus sending from our Catholic
homes, into the arena of public life, not partisans but patri-
ots."[29] The purposes of both Catholic and public historical lessons were identical in spirit, but Catholic schoolmen wanted
American Catholic children to be proud of both components of

---

29. The Little Bee (Chicago) #1 (December 1884); Sadlier's
Excelsior Studies in the History of the United States for Schools
(New York, 1879).

their heritage. Young Catholics were to render their spiritual loyalty to the Catholic Church and their temporal loyalty to the United States.

Textbooks are only one indication of the values taught in the public and the Catholic classroom, yet they provide a good impression of those values. Thus, the similarity between the two collections of books is cause for speculation. Even though the Catholic schools remained distinct from public schools in some areas -- intensive religious and foreign language instruction, for example -- they became increasingly similar in social content throughout the nineteenth century. "The parish schools came into existence not only to further the Catholic faith," noted Howard Weisz, "but also to serve as a surrogate for the public schools. Pressure to emulate those public schools came from parents jealous of the educational advantages of others."[30] The values implicit in Catholic texts reflected the increasing Americanization of the Irish and German population. Perhaps the similarities between public and Catholic schoolbooks is the best evidence of that fact.

---

30. Howard D. Weisz, "Irish American Attitudes and the Americanization of the English Language Parochial School," New York History 53 (April 1972): 175.

CHAPTER VIII

THE SEARCH FOR ORDER IN CATHOLIC PAROCHIAL EDUCATION

I

Catholic parochial education experienced something of a revolution in the years from 1880 to 1930. Diversity and experimen-
tation had been the chief characteristics of Catholic educational
development throughout most of the nineteenth century. The nature and extent of parochial education had varied from diocese to
diocese and even from parish to parish within each diocese. But
by 1880, American society was placing an increased emphasis on
the importance of formal education and Catholic leaders soon
realized that the status quo would not be acceptable to Catholic
parents in the new century. If Catholic schools were not competitive, Catholic parents would send their children to public
schools. Thus bishops, pastors, and parents alike called for reform in Catholic education and a forthright commitment to excellence. "Our objective," noted the editor of one diocesan paper,
"is to place Catholic schools not only on an equality with public
schools, but [also] to elevate [them] to such a standard of efficiency as will make them objects of envy to our non-Catholic
neighbors."[1]

---

1. Western Catholic, February 23, 1884. The search for order
in Catholic education was one part of a general organizational
revolution in American society during these decades. This trend

With this objective in mind, the American bishops took deci-
sive action on parochial education when they met at the Third
Plenary Council of Baltimore in November 1884. In fact, the education decrees laid down at Baltimore were something of a blue-
print for parochial school development over the next fifty years.
Not enough can be said about the importance of these decrees in
bringing order to Catholic parochial education. "Everyone acquainted at all with the history of Catholic schools in the
United States," notes historian Philip Gleason, "knows that the
Third Plenary Council of Baltimore was a major milestone in their
development."[2]

The actions that distinguished this council from previous
meetings was the shift in tone of the pastoral decrees from the
language of exhortation to the language of command. For the
first time, the bishops specifically required pastors to establish and maintain parish schools and instructed Catholic parents
to send their children to these institutions. There were some
exceptions, of course, but the language was unequivocal -- support parochial education or face disciplinary action. After more
than thirty years of exhortation, the hierarchy had run out of
patience.

---

has been analyzed masterfully by Robert H. Weibe in his book, The
Search for Order, 1877-1920 (New York, 1967).

2. Philip Gleason, "Baltimore III and Education," U.S.
Catholic Historian 4 (1985): 273; Francis P. Cassidy, "Catholic
Education in the Third Plenary Council of Baltimore," Catholic
Historical Review 34 (October 1948): 257-305 and (January 1949):
414-436; Bernard J. Meiring, Educational Aspects of the
Legislation of the Councils of Baltimore (New York, 1978).

The bishops were well aware that intimidation was not the way to win the laity over to parochial education. The Catholic school system would not last unless its institutions were equal in quality to public schools. In eight additional decrees, "concerning the ways and means of improving the parochial schools," the hierarchy called for the establishment of diocesan boards of school examiners, the creation of normal schools for the training of sister-teachers and lay teachers, and the implementation of competency tests to insure teacher excellence. Pastors were called upon to take course work in pedagogy and psychology, and encouraged to teach religion classes themselves. The laity in general and parents in particular were encouraged to become more active in the work of the parish schools. "Little of this ambitious program was put into effect immediately," adds Gleason, "but it helped to shape the systemization of parochial education that took place over the next generation."[3]

The strong language in the education decrees gave needed momentum to efforts to expand and improve parochial schools. Many bishops returned to their dioceses determined to bring order to their patchwork of parish-based schools. The highest priority was given to the expansion of the school system into every parish and, over the next twenty-five years, both the number and the enrollment of Catholic parochial schools nearly doubled. Second priority was given to the establishment of diocesan school boards and by 1910 a solid majority of dioceses would establish such boards. Third, the bishops encouraged in-service training for

3. Gleason, "Baltimore III and Education," p. 274.

both lay and religious teachers as a means of improving the quality of classroom instruction. These three initiatives characterized the first three decades of the Catholic education revolution
from 1885 to 1915.[4]

The emergence of a new generation of bishops in the first
two decades of the twentieth century marked the beginning of a
second period of reform in the years from 1915 to 1930. This
second campaign was not a formal one, however. It was the result
of a collective management style of new prelates who were determined to manage their dioceses with the utmost economy and efficiency. To do so required greater centralization of authority
over all diocesan institutions including the schools. This trend
was particularly evident in the larger dioceses, the hometowns of
the majority of American Catholics. Unlike the generation that
had preceded them, these new bishops were American-born and
Vatican-educated, men who served long tenures devoted to raising
the visibility of the Church in the United States. They hoped to
bring the Church in general, and parochial schools in particular,
greater prestige and self-esteem.[5]

---

4. The best discussion of the first stage of the Catholic edu-
cational revolution can be found in James W. Sanders, The
Education of an Urban Minority: Catholics in Chicago, 1833-1965
(New York, 1977). See particularly, Chapter Nine, "Order Out of
Chaos," pp. 141-147.

5. For a thoughtful discussion of the second stage of the
Catholic education revolution, see Edward R. Kantowicz, "Cardinal
Mundelein of Chicago: A Consolidating Bishop," in David J.
Alvarez, ed., An American Church (Morega, Calif., 1979), 63-72;
and Kantowicz, Corporation Sole: Cardinal Mundelein and Chicago
Catholicism (Notre Dame, 1983), pp. 1-8.

Chicago and Milwaukee are two useful case studies of the Catholic revolution in the years from 1880 to 1930. By the turn of the century these two growing archdioceses were between them educating almost 10 percent of all the children enrolled in Catholic parochial schools in the United States. The archbishops of these two cities faced typical problems in trying to bring order to the chaotic growth of the last two decades of the old century and the first decades of the new. "Their leadership and that of similar bishops in other cities, plus the growing number and wealth of Catholics," notes historian Edward R. Kantowicz, "achieved separate but equal status for the Catholic Church in the United States. Inheriting a strong institutional base and morally intransigent faith, the twentieth century bishops 'put the Church on the map' and got it 'out of the catacombs' by providing highly visible leadership and instilling pride and confidence in American Catholics."[6] The transformation of the Catholic school system from a localized patchwork of parish schools into a national network of diocesan systems was a major part of this effort.

II

Archbishop Patrick Feehan faced an enormous task when he returned to Chicago from the council at Baltimore. Parochial schools had been operated on the parish level in Chicago since the establishment of the diocese in 1843, but there was little

---

6. Kantowicz, "Cardinal Mundelein and the Shaping of Twentieth Century Catholicism," Journal of American History 68 (June 1981): 68.

order or pattern in this development. One parish might have a half a dozen schools taught by two or more religious orders, while the parish next door might have no school at all.

Even those parishes that did have schools did not communicate with each other; in fact, many parishes seemed to compete with one another for prospective pupils. "Since each parish formed its own school," notes historian James Sanders, "the parishioners and pastors strove mightily to outdo their neighbors in the quest for glory. The parish's school plant and its educational program gave testimony to the generosity, prosperity, and interest of its constituents."[7]

This is not to say that parish schools were completely isolated from each other. Schools run by the same religious order had much in common, and parishes of the same ethnic culture maintained lines of communication on educational issues. But whatever order came from these alliances was more than offset by the barriers they created between different religious orders and different ethnic groups. "The inbred peculiarities displayed by religious communities compounded within the parish unit, ethnic separatism, and the unquestioned prerogatives of the parish pastor," adds Sanders, "posed abundant obstacles to centralized control of the schools."[8]

There was no doubt about Feehan's commitment to parochial education. In fact, he chaired the committee of bishops that drafted the education decrees proclaimed at Baltimore. Yet de-

---

7. Sanders, Education of an Urban Minority, pp. 143-144.

8. Ibid., p. 145.

sire as he might to implement the decrees, Feehan understood the realities of educational decision-making in his diocese. The archbishop moved slowly, therefore, not willing to upset the relations he had so carefully established with his pastors. It was not until 1887, at an archdiocesan synod, that Feehan moved to establish a board of school examiners.

At first, the board was more an acknowledgement of the ethnic and educational diversity of the archdiocese than an effort to centralize authority over the schools. "The board consisted of parish priests, one each for the regular territorial parishes of the north, west, and south sides respectively, another for the schools outside Chicago, several for the German schools, one for the French, and another for the Polish and Bohemians."[9] The board encouraged the establishment of new schools and suggested improvements in existing institutions, but the real authority for the schools remained in the hands of the pastors.

This limited role for the board did not please everyone in Chicago. The New World, the archdiocesan paper, reported the centralization efforts of other dioceses and asked why Chicago lagged behind. In 1894 the paper noted the "importance of uniformity" and the following year called for a single normal school for women religious in the diocese and formal pedagogical training for all seminarians.[10] Throughout the 1890s, the paper complained about the lack of consistency from one parish to the

---

9. Ibid., p. 142; Cassidy, "Catholic Education in the Third Plenary Council," passim.

10. The New World, December 22, 1894, May 25, 1895.

next. "It is greatly deplored that we have not a more uniform system," noted one editorial.[11]

A measure of uniformity did come to the diocese by the turn of the century. In 1897, one parish organized a general teacher training institute for women religious that was attended by several hundred sisters. In the 1910s, local Catholic universities -- DePaul and Loyola -- offered education courses that contributed to the growing uniformity. But it was the movement of the laity, from parish to parish within the city and from city to suburb, that contributed most to the growing demand for uniformity. "More than anything else," notes Sanders, "the impact of residential mobility overcame isolation in the local parish, the convent, and the ethnic community. A mobile population seemed to demand a centralized system where children could pass from one school to another with minimum friction."[12]

The pace of centralization increased substantially with the arrival of George Mundelein as archbishop in 1916. Mundelein succeeded the kindly James Quigley who had conducted a status quo administration as archbishop in the years from 1902 to 1916. It was Mundelein who succeeded in centralizing authority over the parochial schools of Chicago, a task far beyond the skills of Feehan or Quigley.

In preparation for his new assignment, Mundelein studied maps of Chicago and examined financial reports from every parish. He immediately grasped the enormity of the problems that he

---

11. Ibid., May 25, 1895.

12. Sanders, Education of an Urban Minority, p. 147.

faced. Chicago was a sprawling archdiocese that had been administered for seventy-five years on the parish level. Mundelein
knew that the challenge was to introduce uniformity and standardization in the archdiocese; more importantly, he knew that he
would have to centralize the responsibility for Church affairs in
Chicago.[13]

One of the major problems was the so-called parochial school
"system." Simply stated, each parish operated its school independently. "The pastors hired the sisters, negotiated their salaries, and built and maintained the school buildings; the sisters
decided what to teach and how to go about it. The bishop, though
he had, theoretically, complete authority over Catholic education, had no real control."[14] Mundelein faced the same old educational patchwork as his predecessors. There was more uniformity in the textbooks, curriculum, and teaching methods among the
schools of one religious order spread across the country than
among the schools of different parishes in Chicago. Mundelein
knew that the situation had to change.

One of Mundelein's first actions on arriving in Chicago was
the appointment of three pastors -- one Irish, one German, one
Polish -- to act as a revitalized board of supervisors over the
parish schools. At the first of his annual clergy conferences,
he explained that the purpose of the board was to coordinate "the
various educational institutions of the Archdiocese into one uni-

---

13. Kantowicz, Corporation Sole, pp. 10-98.

14. Ibid., p. 85.

form and efficient educational system."[15] It was a clear statement of the new archbishop's educational goals.

The archbishop moved with remarkable speed. By the autumn
of 1916, the board had succeeded in developing a plan that required the use of English for all subjects except religion and
reading, and provided for a common textbook selection for every
school. "Gradually," notes historian Edward R. Kantowicz, "uniformity was extended to other school matters as well, such as a
common salary schedule for teaching sisters and uniform final
exams in all schools. Though the schools remained decentralized
and parochial, in the sense that the parish pastors retained responsibility for finances and for hiring sisters, Mundelein's
school board went a long way toward providing a common Catholic
education in all parish schools."[16] There was some grumbling
from the Polish parishes, but no pastor challenged Mundelein's
plan.

American involvement in World War I generated concerns about
the foreign loyalties of some American Catholics. Of particular
concern was the content of parochial education and Mundelein,
along with his fellow bishops, defended their Catholic school
system. Mundelein wrote to former president Theodore Roosevelt.
"I need not tell you, of course," he wrote, "that there is hardly
any institution here in the country that does so much to bring
about a sure, safe, and sane Americanization of immigrant people

---

15. The New World, March 31, 1916; Sanders, Education of an
Urban Minority, p. 148.

16. Kantowicz, Corporation Sole, p. 16.

as do our parochial schools. My endeavor always will be to keep them up to the highest standard possible so that they may be my monument rather than costly churches after I have gone and the children that come from them be every bit as good American citizens as they are Catholics."[17]   But Mundelein found his time taken up with war-related activities, and he was not able to complete his centralization plan for the parochial schools until the 1920s.

After the war, Mundelein was able to solidify the power of his school board through the appointment of co-superintendents. After a year of training at the Catholic University of America, Fathers John Ford and John Kozlowski took over the daily operations of the school board. Thus, by 1920, Mundelein had in place all of the elements of his plan to centralize the schools. "Standardization of elementary schools," wrote the archbishop that year, "is to be effected this year through the work of trained inspectors working in conjunction with or under the direction of the diocesan board of education and aided by an advisory committee of practical educators selected, one each, from the forty-six educational communities of the archdiocese."[18]   It was a practical system that allowed for some diversity among and between the various teaching orders and ethnic groups.

The plan worked well for three years. But the retirement of Ford due to illness, and his replacement by Father Henry

---

17. Mundelein to Roosevelt, June 5, 1916, copy in the AAC; Kantowicz, Corporation Sole, p. 25.

18. The New World September 10, 1920; Sanders, Education of an Urban Minority, p. 151.

Matimore, led to an intense intra-diocesan controversy that underscored the fragile nature of Mundelein's system. Matimore challenged the balance of power that existed between the board, the teaching orders, and the parishes; he insisted on centralized management, visited all of the schools personally, issued bulletins to the teachers on pedagogy, and sent elaborate semi-annual reports to the archbishop.

Matimore was a tireless worker, eager to improve the system, but he was not politically astute and he offended the board. By 1924, Matimore was prohibited by the board from visiting the schools and ordered to submit his reports to the board, not the archbishop. He also was prohibited from meeting with parochial school teachers unless he had the expressed permission of the board. Matimore was crushed by these restrictions, and from that time on played no significant role in the educational affairs of the archdiocese. Finally, in 1926, he was dismissed as superintendent.[19]

The archbishop gave no reason for the dismissal, but it was clear to everyone that the young superintendent had moved too far too fast. "Matimore's failure," noted Sanders, "stemmed above all from his inability to understand and cope with the social realities in Chicago. As a result, despite his considerable expertise, he alienated almost everyone -- ethnic groups, sisters, the school board, and pastors."[20]   Mundelein learned that he

19. Sanders, Education of an Urban Minority, pp. 152-157; Kantowicz, Corporation Sole, pp. 88-89.

20. Sanders, Education of an Urban Minority, p. 154.

needed a superintendent who was as much a politician as a professional educator. To replace Matimore, Mundelein selected the af-
fable Father Daniel Cunningham who reestablished the equilibrium
of the early years of the decade. Cunningham knew the limits of
Mundelein's educational plan.

By the end of the decade the parochial schools of Chicago
did form a bona fide system. They shared a uniform curriculum,
common textbooks, and a standardized testing system to evaluate
student achievement. The board resolved differences that arose
between pastors and teaching orders. It was everything that
Mundelein hoped for when he introduced the plan in 1916. Most
importantly, Mundelein had completed a task begun by Feehan fifty
years earlier. Mundelein had achieved the systemization and order that had eluded Chicago's parochial schools for so long.

III

Archbishop Michael Heiss did not need the decrees of the
Third Plenary Council to spur him to take action on Milwaukee's
parish schools. Indeed, throughout his episcopal career, Heiss
was obsessed with a desire to establish a school in every parish
in his archdiocese and to centralize his authority over the
schools. Evidence of this desire came shortly after Heiss arrived in Milwaukee to succeed the beloved John Martin Henni.
Among his first acts, the new archbishop sent out to his parishes
a circular letter that stressed the need for parochial schools
and instructed pastors not to absolve parents who refused to pa-
tronize parish schools. Even though few pastors enforced this

controversial policy, the instruction was an indication of the new archbishop's zealous interest in education.[21]

In the summer of 1881, Heiss tried yet another tactic to increase school attendance. On August 28, the archbishop announced that the confirmation of all Catholic children had to be preceded by at least one year's attendance in a Catholic school. Heiss action was not original; in fact, it had been Vatican policy since 1875, and had been in force in the German parishes of Milwaukee for several years, but the extension of the policy to the English-speaking parishes made it news.

The Milwaukee Sentinel felt compelled to editorialize on the matter. "Perhaps on further consideration," urged the editors, "the Archbishop may conclude that the practice of the venerable Henni to the matter was wise for the present generations well as for his own and may deem it best, hereafter, as heretofore, to allow the rule to sleep until some pressing occasion shall arise to demand an awakening."[22] There was little reaction from the laity recorded in the press and the issue was of no concern to the Sentinel after its editorial.

The Catholic Citizen, however, was a tireless champion of the archbishop and his educational initiatives. By 1883, "efficiency" had become the byword on parochial education. "In the end," went one typical editorial, "the success or failure of all schools is determined by their efficiency . . . . all true

---

21. Benjamin Blied, Three Archbishops (Milwaukee, 1955), p. 28.

22. Milwaukee Sentinel, August 30, 1881.

friends of our Catholic parish schools feel that efficiency and thoroughness are the only real conditions of permanent useful- ness."[23] Nothing would hide the deficiencies of a poor school. "Laxity of discipline, want of a system and neglect of a thorough and studious habit will be apparent." Good teachers made the school efficient and the Catholic Citizen advocated higher stan- dards and better pay for parochial school teachers.

The archbishop's next step was to organize a school board in 1883 "to examine prospective teachers for Catholic schools, to regulate courses of study, and to promote high standards of edu- cation generally."[24] Heiss also encouraged his pastors to estab- lish parish school societies to raise money to underwrite the cost of the schools. The establishment of the board and the sug- gestion of school societies were not passive gestures on Heiss' part. The archbishop went so far as to serve as the ex officio chairman of the school board, and he sought and received papal approbation for the school societies.

Encouraged by Heiss actions, the Catholic Citizen bragged about the quality of Catholic education. "The natural advantages of a Catholic school system are however worth nothing unless in- telligently developed . . . . There must too be added efficiency in this line of work wherein Catholic education comes more di- rectly in competition with the secular schools, viz: secular edu-

---

23. The Catholic Citizen, August 25, 1883.

24. M. Mileta Ludwig, Right Hand Glove Uplifted: The Life of the Right Reverend Michael Heiss (New York, 1968), pp. 452-453.

cation."[25]   These comments were something of a preface to the Citizen's proposal for a national system of school boards.   It would be the Milwaukee system writ large.

In June of 1884, the Citizen outlined a rationale and a list of duties for the board. "Our schools must be systemized," wrote the editors, "that we may realize the best results from them and the sooner that is done the better for the schools. In each diocese, let a diocesan board be organized that shall have the management of all the parochial schools therein. A uniform course of study throughout the diocese would enable a pupil to continue his studies without interruption in the event that he moved from one parish to another . . . . The whole school work should be so determined as to clearly indicate how much pupils must accomplish in each branch every year that they are in attendance and so indicate at what stage of their advancement new studies should be commenced."[26]   The Citizen also advocated dividing each diocese into districts, with each one supervised by a member of the central school board. The plan would insure that each child would receive "sufficient" instruction in all of the essential branches of American education and that the dictates of the school board were obeyed.[27]

Heiss also was one of the most active proponents of a national plan for parochial education. He saw the Third Plenary Council as an opportunity to implement such a plan and, along

---

25. The Catholic Citizen, May 3, 1884.

26. Ibid., June 14, 1884.

27. Ibid.

with other American archbishops, he journeyed to Rome to develop the agenda for the forthcoming council. In the course of these discussions, Heiss argued that the public school was a proximate danger to the faith of Catholics. Once again he offered his plan to allow confessors to withhold the sacrament of penance from parents who did not send their children to parish schools. Other archbishops demurred from this plan, however, and this tactic did not materialize in the council agenda.

Heiss did not abandon his zealous commitment to parish schools, however. At the council meeting itself, he argued for strong language in the education decrees. He wanted his brother bishops to "command" parents to send their children to parochial schools. Once again, his colleagues balked at such strong language. It was with reluctance that Heiss accepted the council's language and after returning to Milwaukee, he moved to implement the decrees to the maximum extent possible.

The actions taken at the Third Plenary Council were applauded by the Catholic Citizen. The bishops had stated clearly that every parish must establish a school except under extraordinary circumstances. Moreover, the council had recommended that every diocese establish a school board for the central administration of the schools. "Raising the standard of Catholic education is no meaningless verbiage," the Citizen noted. "It means the creation of a more efficient, popular, and practical ideal. It means a consistent ideal to approximate this high ideal. It precludes self-satisfaction, stagnation, and retrogressiveness. It means that the barnacle must go and the dead wood must be cut off."[28]

Heiss died in the autumn of 1890 to be succeeded by Frederic X. Katzer, the Bishop of Green Bay. There is no doubt that Heiss would have been pleased with the appointment; the two men shared a strong commitment to the future of parochial education. Just prior to his appointment to Milwaukee, Katzer had led the successful campaign against the detested Bennett Law which required the use of English in all classrooms, both in public and in private schools. Here there is a question of principle, the principle of state control," Katzer wrote in the midst of the campaign. "If we grant this to the state than it also can prescribe -- and it will no doubt do it -- that we can teach English and nothing else. Foolish people go so far as to allow the state to meddle with family affairs. Accordingly, we will next get state commissioners who will dictate to the housewife what she could cook."[29] Katzer served in the place of the aging and infirm Heiss in this critical campaign.

Katzer was, therefore, a logical but somewhat unpopular candidate to succeed Heiss. After two German-born prelates, many English-speaking Catholics in Milwaukee and around the country were hoping that an American would be appointed to the post. A majority of the American archbishops agreed, but their petitions to Rome went unanswered. The Vatican wanted a German in Milwau-

---

28. Ibid., December 20, 1884.

29. Die Columbia, May 29, 1890; Milwaukee Sentinel, May 28, 1890; Blied, Three Archbishops, p. 54.

kee and Katzer got the job. His leadership style was similar to that of Heiss. "His administration of the archdiocese," notes one biographer, "was characterized by a uniform regard for justice and an adherence to the laws of the Church."[30]

Katzer was particularly zealous in enforcing the education decrees of the Third Plenary Council. He pushed for more schools and vigorously opposed any compromise with public education. In 1895, as he was making his regular visit to Rome required of all bishops, Katzer assessed the progress of his diocese in educational affairs. He was pleased to report to the pope that his flock had been particularly good about obeying the education decrees of the Baltimore council. He acknowledged some failures, but also offered the hope of further progress. In summation, Katzer noted why he thought education was so important. "A parish with no Catholic school is half a thing," he wrote, "and in a parish whose members do not show a warm interest in a parochial school, Catholic life is lacking . . . . A child which does not attend a Catholic school is deprived of the means of being adequately instructed and reared in its holy religion."[31] The Catholic school was the single most important institution in preserving the religious faith of children.

Katzer became seriously ill in March 1903, but continued to work on educational matters. In May, he signed papers that formally incorporated the archdiocese, and about the same time, he

---

30. Dictionary of American Biography (New York, 1932), s.v. "Katzer, Frederic Xavier."

31. Quoted in Blied, Three Archbishops, p. 70.

authorized the publication of a booklet that standardized classroom instruction and textbook selection throughout the archdiocese. Katzer had previously appointed a group of clergymen to
develop the plan that limited the educational authority of local
pastors and brought substantial uniformity to Milwaukee's parochial schools. The booklet was to be Katzer's last contribution
to the centralization of parochial education. He died in July
1903.

Katzer was succeeded by Sebastian G. Messmer, yet another
German who had served as bishop of Green Bay. Messmer also
shared his predecessor's concern for parochial education and
during his twenty-six years as archbishop of Milwaukee, he would
build more than forty new parish schools. Messmer had come to
Milwaukee with a proven track record on educational matters. As
bishop of Green Bay, he vigorously applied the Baltimore decrees
to the letter.

Very early in his tenure, Messmer began a campaign to further tighten diocesan authority over parochial education. His
first, and many say foremost, contribution to the centralization
effort was the preparation and publication of the Handbook for
Catholic Parishioners in 1907. The 126-page book was both a parish operations manual and a catechetical guide. The first part
of the book discussed parish incorporation, the salaries of
pastors and curates, and similarly mundane matters. The handbook
also discussed liturgical matters such as the use of music in the
Mass and the religious instruction of children and their preparation to receive the sacraments. The booklet was an important

step in codifying the decrees that Heiss and Katzer had promul-
gated.

The handbook offered specific instruction on the operation
of parish schools. Messmer encouraged parishes to establish
local school boards composed of laymen and chaired by the pastor.
The archbishop also used the handbook to encourage the establishment of parish libraries for use by the students.

Messmer handed down strict guidelines on school expendi-
tures. "School money, if there must be such, should be as low as
possible," noted the handbook, "it should not be collected by the
teachers, whose dignity suffers by such practice. Let the parents, not the children, pay it directly to the secretary of the
parish unless a special collector be appointed for the purpose.
The schoolbooks and stationery should be bought by the parish;
but whether bought by the parish or the priest or sisters, they
must be sold to the children for exactly the same price as bought
from the publishers. For more than one reason it is poor policy
to make up the teachers' salary by overcharging the children for
books and stationery."[32] Along with the diocesan school board
established by Heiss, and the curriculum and textbook policy
established by Katzer, Messmer provided a substantial measure of
uniformity to the parish schools of Milwaukee.

Over the next decade Messmer continued to tighten his control over parish schools. But it was the First World War, with
its anti-German hysteria, that put Messmer to the test. On Janu-

---

32. Handbook for Catholic Parishioners (Milwaukee, 1907),
p. 60.

ary 1, 1917, Messmer ordered that all parish records would henceforth be kept in English, and that the schools were to stress
their commitment to American values. Messmer refused "to allow
the impression go out that the public schools are the only
schools where true patriotism and loyal duty to the country are
being cultivated."[33]

The war, with its attendant emphasis on Americanism, assisted Messmer in bringing English to the last of the die-hard
German and Polish Catholic classrooms. By the mid 1920s, it was
clear that the once German diocese of Milwaukee was shedding its
European flavor to become fully American. More importantly, the
last of the differences between ethnic Catholic and American
Catholic parish schools were disappearing. The homogenization of
parochial education in Milwaukee had been the culmination of a
fifty-year process. The credit for the campaign goes equally to
archbishops Heiss, Katzer, and Messmer.

IV

The Catholic education revolution was one important aspect
of the general transformation within the American Church that
took place in the last decades of the nineteenth and the early
decades of the twentieth centuries. The new century had brought
forth a new generation of bishops who were determined to give the
Church self-confidence and clout within American society. "Most
of them built or expanded seminaries in their dioceses, reorga-
nized their central administrations, collected large sums for the

_____

33. Quoted in Blied, Three Archbishops, p. 137.

Pope, the Propagation of the Faith and local charitable works, and exercised political influence both publicly and privately."[34] Both George Mundelein and Sebastian Messmer were of this generation, and among their most significant achievements was the establishment of order over the parochial schools of their respective dioceses.

The Great Depression of the 1930s brought a halt to the organizational revolution in Catholic parochial education. Most dioceses, including Chicago and Milwaukee, focused their energies on the considerable task of keeping the schools open. New plans for more centralization and uniformity would have to wait for better times. Yet, in looking back over the previous five decades, Church leaders and educators could feel proud of all that they had accomplished. In the years since the Third Plenary Council, the parochial educational establishment had transformed itself from a diocesan confederation of autonomous parish schools into a national system of Catholic education.

---

34. Kantowicz, "Cardinal Mundelein and the Shaping of Twentieth Century Catholicism," p. 68.

CONCLUSION

THREE MYTHS ABOUT AMERICAN CATHOLIC EDUCATION

The history of American Catholic parochial education has been caught up in myth and misunderstanding for more than a century. The confusion has been due to several factors, but two stand out as the major causes. Certainly the lack of serious historical scholarship on the topic has been a major problem. The filiopietism of James A. Burns and succeeding generations of Catholic educational historians has clouded both the scholarly and the popular understanding of the contours of Catholic education. So also, the critics of Catholic education have added to the confusion by mixing polemics with scholarship. Groups such as Americans United for the Separation of Church and State and Americans for Religious Liberty have cast aspersions on the value of parochial education in the protracted debate over public funding for private schools. It is somewhat ironic that an institution as familiar as the local parish school could be so misunderstood.

Over the years three myths have come to dominate the popular understanding of the origins and evolution of Catholic parochial education. The first is that Catholics responded uniformly to the campaign for parish schools. "The story of the first Catholic schools in Milwaukee and Chicago," argued Burns, "recalls the

early history of New York, Baltimore, and Boston."[1]   Burns had no
documentary evidence for his claim, but it was easy to accept his
hypothesis because the American Church in the early twentieth
century presented an image of centralized authority and uniform
belief.   Indeed, the very word "catholic," commonly translated as
"universal," underscored the claim that the Catholic Church spoke
and acted as one.   Under such circumstances, it is not surprising
that most interested individuals -- non-Catholics as well as
Catholics -- believed that the history of Catholic education was
virtually the same from one diocese to the next.

But such claims of uniformity were without much basis in
fact.   To the contrary, the existing documentation on the diocesan level points to variations in the educational experiences of
Catholics, variations that were almost limitless during the nineteenth century.   In communities as distant and different from one
another as Savannah, Georgia, is from Fairbault, Minnesota, or
Lowell, Massachusetts, Catholic schools were part of the public
school system.   Teachers were paid with public funds and local
parishes received rent money for the use of school buildings.
But in large eastern cities such as New York and Philadelphia,
Catholic schools formed systems unto themselves and there was
only minimal contact between public and Catholic schoolmen.   In
still other communities -- Chicago and Milwaukee for example --
the history of Catholic parochial education fit somewhere between
these two points on the spectrum.   In short, there was no single

----

1. James A. Burns, The Growth and Development of the Catholic
School System in the United States (New York, 1912), p. 15.

parochial school experience and certainly no national system of Catholic education in the United States.

A second myth revolves around the educational content of the Catholic school curriculum. Critics of parochial education have argued that parish schools have been fundamentally divisive because they preserved ethnic and religious traditions at the expense of American values. This was a persuasive argument largely because Catholic education differed from public education in several highly visible ways. Many Catholic classrooms were staffed by women in distinctive religious garb who spoke in foreign languages and broken English. In addition, classroom walls were covered with religious illustrations and statues. Catholic criticism of the very concept of the common school created additional acrimony and concern. It was logical to assume, therefore, that the content of Catholic education was foreign to the American way.

But this myth was based almost entirely on form rather than substance. If one uses Catholic schoolbooks and curricula as evidence, it is clear that the message of Catholic parochial education has always been decidedly American. In fact, the Catholic curriculum emphasized the same values that were taught in public schools. To be sure, there was a greater emphasis on moral and religious issues, but Catholic teachers also stressed patriotism, diligence, and deference to authority among other traditional values taught in public schools. Historians such as Sam Bass Warner and Timothy L. Smith have documented the flag-waving pa-

triotism of parochial education."[2]   "The goal of literacy, both
Catholic and secular, for any child who presented himself at the
school door," notes Warner, "meant that the Catholic Church was
as securely tied to the task of Americanization through education
as were the contemporary public schools."[3]

A third myth is that bishops were united in their support
for parish schools, that they were the principal leaders of the
parochial school movement, and that the laity followed the bishops in lock-step fashion.   "Catholic immigrants did not need to
be convinced of the necessity of Catholic schools," wrote Father
Burns.   "They were of one mind with their pastors and bishops on
the subject."[4]   Burns based his claim on the presumption that the
frequent episcopal pastorals on education had a substantive impact on the parish level.   Since Burns accepted the hypothesis
that the response to Catholic education was uniform, it is not
surprising that he also believed that the hierarchy was united on
this issue and that it led the parochial school movement.   In
tightly structured bureaucracies, uniformity is expected and
leadership comes from the top down.

---

2. Sam Bass Warner, The Urban Wilderness (New York, 1972),
pp. 161-166, 175-176; Timothy L. Smith, "Immigrant Social
Aspirations and American Education, 1880-1930," American
Quarterly 21 (Fall 1969): 523-543; Smith, "Parochial Education
and American Culture," History and Education, edited by Paul
Nash, (New York, 1970), pp. 192-211; and Howard Weisz, Irish
American and Italian American Educational Views and Activities,
1870-1900 (New York, 1976).

3. Warner, Urban Wilderness, p. 166.

4. Burns, Growth and Development, p. 16.

But Catholic bishops, pastors, and parents were not docile sheep. In fact, a number of pastors and bishops gave parochial education a low priority in their parishes and dioceses; many Catholic parents openly resisted the campaign for parish schools. They found the public schools perfectly acceptable for their children.

Of course, many Catholic parents did support parochial schools but even then, they did not always follow the lead of their bishops. To the contrary, the day-to-day leadership of the parochial school movement came from coalitions of pastors, sister-teachers, and committed parents working together to establish schools that would appeal to a majority of Catholics in their neighborhoods. "Because the building and financing of its schools rested with the families of the parish," notes Sam Bass Warner, "the values of the Church itself became tied to the hopes and values of child-rearing which its neighborhood supporters possessed."[5] This is not to say that the bishops were not among the leaders of the parish school movement, but it was the participation of priests and people that was the key to its success.

The history of Catholic schooling in Chicago and Milwaukee belies the myths that have so dominated both the popular and the scholarly understanding of parochial education. First, available documentary evidence points to the distinctive aspects of the development of parochial education in the Midwest generally and in Chicago and Milwaukee specifically. It was no mere replay of the experience of Bishop Hughes and the Catholic community in New

5. Warner, Urban Wilderness, p. 166.

York. Second, parochial classroom instruction in these two communities was decidedly American in tone and content, even in the
ethnic parishes. In fact, Catholic schoolmen went so far as to
argue that their institutions were closer to the ideals of the
Founding Fathers than the public schools because parish schools
sustained the moral values on which the country was founded.
Third, the parochial education movement in Chicago and Milwaukee
was not the exclusive domain of the hierarchy, nor was the
response uniform from one bishop to the next. Bishop Hughes may
have been boss in New York, but the bishops of Chicago and Milwaukee learned to work closely with pastors, mother-superiors,
and the laity to shape the parish schools. In sum, Catholic education in Chicago and Milwaukee did not follow the popular sce-
nario laid down by Father Burns and his successors.

Overall, the parochial education movement in Chicago and
Milwaukee is evidence of the failure of religious and educational
historians to take into account the variety of Catholic educational experiences in the United States. These historians have
taken Catholic schooling for granted, using Bishop Hughes and his
New York diocese as a model to describe parochial education
across the nation. But the parochial education movement was not
so much a unified national campaign as it was a collection of independent efforts administered at the local level. Each Catholic
community -- diocese and parish -- has its own history which cannot be ignored if we are to have an accurate portrait of Catholic
parochial education in the United States.

Most importantly, the history of Catholic education in Chicago, Milwaukee, and other big cities underscores the constantly changing nature of Catholicism in American urban society. Even though it claimed to be immutable and unchanging, the Church in the United States was adapting to almost constant change in the years from 1840 to 1930. "The fact is," noted David J. O'Brien almost twenty years ago, "that the hierarchy, clergy, and laity all wished to be both American and Catholic and their attempt to reconcile the two, to mediate between religious and social roles, lies at the heart of the American experience."[6] The local history of Catholic education reveals how each diocese institutionalized the process of achieving these twin goals. It is an important but largely ignored chapter in American history.

---

6. David J. O'Brien, "American Catholicism and the Diaspora," Cross Currents 16 (Summer 1966): 308-309.

ESSAY ON SOURCES

I

Catholicism is one of the oldest traditions in North America. Beginning with the establishment of the parish of St. Augustine in the Spanish colony of Florida in the mid-sixteenth century, the Church has nurtured both the spiritual and material welfare of millions of Americans. The Church is fast approaching the anniversary of 425 years of continuous service in the territory that now forms the continental United States.

It is unfortunate, therefore, that until recently American Catholics in general, and the Church establishment in particular, have done so little to document and tell the story of that service, particularly its extraordinary educational enterprise. In fact, it was not until a century ago, with the establishment of the U. S. Catholic Historical Society in New York, the American Catholic Historical Society in Philadelphia, and the Catholic Archives of America at the University of Notre Dame, that Catholic scholars began to preserve and write about the unique and important history of their Church. For these initial efforts, we have to thank John Gilmary Shea, Martin I. J. Griffin, and James F. Edwards -- men who dedicated their lives to preserving the contributions of Catholicism to the American experience.

As part of their effort, these men documented the attitudes of the Catholic hierarchy toward education. Yet the impact of

these historian/archivists on the general development of American
educational historiography has not been very significant. Catholics have been the "invisible" contributors to the history of
American schooling. The reasons for this lack of influence can
be traced to a severe limitation on the quantity and quality of
historical source materials on Catholic education, as well as to
a tradition of filiopietism among Catholic educational historians.

II

The quantity and quality of primary source materials on
Catholic schooling in the nineteenth century are as varied as the
educational experiences themselves. For some archdioceses -- New
York, Philadelphia, and Baltimore are three -- the record is
quite complete. But for other dioceses there are few materials.
The Archives of the Archdiocese of Boston, for example, has less
than 1,600 items on all aspects of Catholicism in that city for
the years from its establishment as a diocese in 1808 to 1907.
It is some what ironic that a denomination with a reputation for
bureaucracy and canon law would do such an uneven job of preserving the documentation of its work.

This is not to say that all Catholic bishops in the nineteenth century were insensitive to the value of archives and records. Many bishops directed their pastors to prepare annual reports describing both the spiritual and financial condition of
their parishes. James Roosevelt Bayley, as bishop of Newark,
went so far as to order his pastors to purchase and use "a good,

strongly-bound Blank Book" to record parish activities. He went on to warn these men that "habitual or willful neglect" of this practice "will be considered a sufficient cause for removal of any pastor." Yet the orders of bishops were not always obeyed and the quantity and quality of records vary substantially from parish to parish.

The variations in documentation are also due to the attitudes of the bishops and the administrative structures that they developed. Boston is a good example of the uneven quality of documentary materials from one bishop to the next. Jean Cheverus, the first bishop of Boston, created few records, an indication of the simplified structure of official Church administration. The second bishop, Benedict Fenwick, was an assiduous creator and preserver of records; he began the practice of keeping a daily journal and even wrote a monograph on the early history of the diocese. Fenwick's successor, John Fitzpatrick, continued the journal but in some what of a desultory fashion; as a result, there are gaps in the Fitzpatrick record. But the relationship between the bishop's personality and the creation of records is most evident in the tenure of Fitzpatrick's successor, John Williams. Even though Williams compiled and preserved a substantial quantity of records, few reveal much about the bishop himself. "He seems to have been reluctant to commit his thoughts to paper," concludes Archdiocesan archivist James O'Toole. The uneven nature of the documentation for Boston is not unique; in fact, it is rather typical.

Researchers should not be surprised, therefore, to learn
that the documentation for the Archdioceses of Chicago and
Milwaukee is in the Boston tradition. The unpublished documentation on Church activities in nineteenth century Chicago and Milwaukee is slim. The problem of finding adequate manuscript material is further compounded by the small amount of information
on the many sister-teachers who taught in the parish schools of
these dioceses. Much of the early history of Catholic education
in these two cities must be written from printed primary sources
such as diocesan newspapers.

There are fewer than one hundred manuscript items on Chicago
diocesan affairs for the years from the establishment of the diocese in 1843 until 1890, making Chicago something of a disaster
in the annals of diocesan record-keeping practices. The first
two bishops -- William Quarter and James Van de Velde -- maintained personal diaries that are the most important sources for
the histories of their short tenures. The third bishop, Anthony
O'Regan, ended the practice, and none of his successors thought
to reestablish the practice. Compounding the record-keeping
problems were the frequent changes of administration, the Chicago
fire of 1871, and the lack of a suitable repository for storing
records. Yet even when the archdiocese stabilized under Patrick
Feehan, few records were preserved, and the few items that were
saved ended up in damp basements and suffered extensive deterioration. An archives was not established for the archdiocese until
the 1950s. Under the direction of Cardinal Joseph Bernardin, the

Archdiocese has refurbished and expanded its archival program, an effort applauded by historians and archivists alike.

It is printed primary sources that are most important to the historiography of Catholic education in Chicago in the nineteenth century. Of particular value are the three diocesan newspapers published during the century: The Western Tablet (1852-1853); The Western Catholic (1869-1890); and The New World (1890 and after). It is in the pages of these weeklies that researchers will find the views of both leaders and lay people on the matter of parochial education.

Also of value are several nineteenth century commemorative volumes that preserve copies of documents that are no longer available in the original. Of particular value are two volumes by James J. McGovern: The Life and Writings of the Reverend John McMullen, D.D. (Chicago, 1888) and Souvenir of the Silver Jubilee in the Episcopacy of His Grace, Patrick A. Feehan (Chicago, 1891).

The unpublished source materials on the Archdiocese of Milwaukee in the nineteenth century are more plentiful than those for Chicago, but barely adequate. There are approximately one thousand pieces covering the years from 1843 until 1890 in the Archives of the Archdiocese of Milwaukee and the library of St. Francis de Sales Seminary, but much of this material is incoming correspondence that reveals very little about Milwaukee Catholicism. This bleak situation is relieved, in part, by the valuable work of the late Monsignor Peter Leo Johnson, former professor of history at the seminary and patron of Milwaukee Catholic history.

Johnson collected, translated, and published the outgoing correspondence of Milwaukee's first two archbishops, John Martin Henni
and Michael Heiss. These invaluable translations, found in the
pages of the seminary quarterly, Salesianum, allow researchers to
avoid the difficult problems of working with nineteenth century
German script.

Johnson also translated a select number of letters of German
missionaries in Wisconsin. Of particular note are: "Letters of
the Reverend Albert Inama, O. Praem," Wisconsin Magazine of
History 11 (1927): 77-95, 197-217, 328-354, 437-458; 12 (1928):
58-96; "Letters of the Right Reverend J.M. Henni and the
Reverend Anthony Urbanek," Wisconsin Magazine of History 10
(1926): 66-94. These letters provide useful insights into the
German Catholic clerical mentality.

In spite of Johnson's best efforts, however, researchers
will find that the major source of information on parochial education in Milwaukee is the Catholic press. Weekly issues of Der
Seebote (1865 and after) and Die Columbia (1873 and after) provide the German Catholic perspective. Irish Catholics in the
city expounded their views in the pages of The Star of Bethlehem
(1869-1870), The Catholic Vindicator (1870-1878), The Milwaukee
Catholic Magazine (1875), and The Catholic Citizen (1878 and
after).

III

Both the quantity and the quality of the published historical literature on Catholic education in the United States has

been very poor. Starting with James A. Burns' two volumes, The
Catholic School System: Its Principles, Origin, and Establishment
(New York, 1908) and The Growth and Development of the Catholic
School System in the United States (New York, 1912), there have
been only marginal efforts to write a balanced history of Catho-
lic schooling in this country. For the most part, these efforts
were defensive and filiopietistic, more apologetics than history.
Most have followed the "seed to fruition" thesis laid down by
Burns. The best of these traditional histories are Harold A.
Buetow, Of Singular Benefit: The Story of U. S. Catholic
Education (New York, 1970) and Glen Gabert, Jr., In Hoc Signo? A
Brief History of Catholic Parochial Schools in the United States
(Port Washington, N. Y., 1973).

Catholic educational historiography in the United States was
dominated by Burns until the mid-1960s. This extraordinary hege-
mony has been analyzed by Vincent P. Lannie in his aptly titled
essay, "Church and School Triumphant: The Sources of American
Catholic Educational Historiography," in History of Education
Quarterly 16 (Summer 1976): 131-145. Burns' influence waned
during the 1960s in the midst of the changes brought on by
Vatican II. This new era of freedom and self-examination within
the Church encouraged scholars to explore the history of Catholic
schooling in an unbiased fashion.

Two scholars made substantial contributions to the profes-
sionalization of Catholic educational historiography. In the
late-1950s and throughout the 1960s, Neil G. McCluskey, S.J.,
published three books and numerous essays that helped to reshape

the scholarly approach to Catholic education. McCluskey penetra-
ted the defensive shell around the parochial school historiography of the Burns school. Although his work is a bit dated today,
it has yet to be superseded. See Neil G. McCluskey, The Catholic
Viewpoint on Education (Garden City, N. Y., 1959); Catholic Education in America: A Documentary History (New York, 1964); and
Catholic Education Faces Its Future (Garden City, 1969).

A second scholar who helped to break the filiopietism of the
past was Vincent P. Lannie. Lannie's major contribution was to
provide solid and balanced narratives of important turning points
in the history of Catholic education. See his Public Money and
Parochial Education: Bishop Hughes, Governor Seward and the New
York School Controversy (Cleveland, 1968); Lannie and Bernard
Diethorn, "For the Honor and Glory of God: The Philadelphia Bible
Riots of 1844," History of Education Quarterly 8 (Spring 1968):
44-106; and Lannie, "Alienation in America: The American Catholic
Immigrant in Pre-Civil War America," Review of Politics 32
(September 1970): 503-521.

Lannie also made a substantial contribution to the historiography as the director of a number of first-rate doctoral disser-
tations and as editor of the Notre Dame Journal of Education
(1970-1976). The Spring 1976 issue included several essays by
Lannie and his students. See Lannie, "Sunlight and Twilight:
Unlocking the Catholic Educational Past," pp. 5-17; Norlene M.
Kunkel, "Christian Free Schools: Bernard McQuaid's Nineteenth
Century Plan," pp. 18-27; and Timothy H. Morrisey, "A Controversial Reformer: Archbishop Ireland and His Educational Beliefs,"

pp. 63-75; all in Notre Dame Journal of Education 7 (Spring 1976). Also see James M. McDonnell, "Orestes Brownson, Catholic Schools, Public Schools, and Education -- A Centennial Apprai- sal," Notre Dame Journal of Education 7 (Summer 1976): 101-122.

McCluskey and Lannie were not alone in their efforts to pro- fessionalize Catholic educational history. Essays and chapters by a number of scholars have contributed to the portrait. Fore- most of these essays is Robert D. Cross, "The Origins of the Catholic Parochial Schools in America," American Benedictine Review 16 (June 1965): 194-209. Researchers will also benefit from reading his book The Emergence of Liberal Catholicism in America (Cambridge, 1958). The many essays of Timothy L. Smith are also required reading. Most useful for the study of Catholic education in the nineteenth century are "Parochial Education and American Culture," in Paul Nash, ed., History and Education (New York, 1970), pp. 192-211, and "Protestant Schooling and American Nationality, 1800-1850," Journal of American History 53 (March 1967): 679-69

Several other scholars deserve a special mention. Thomas T. McAvoy , C.S.C., published "Public Schools vs. Catholic Schools and James McMaster," in Review of Politics 28 (January 1966): 19- 46. McAvoy's student, Philip Gleason, published "Immigration and American Catholic Intellectual Life," Review of Politics 26 (April 1964): 147-173. Gleason's new book Keeping the Faith: American Catholicism Past and Present (Notre Dame, 1987) includes the best overview of the educational decrees of the Third Plenary Council of Baltimore. Gleason's colleague at the University of

Notre Dame, Jay P. Dolan, discusses parochial education in his masterful volumes, The Immigrant Church: New York's Irish and German Catholics, 1815-1865 (Baltimore, 1975) and The American Catholic Experience: From Colonial Times to the Present (Garden City, 1985). The latter work includes an excellent chapter on parochial education. Also of value are Howard Weisz, "Irish American Attitudes and the Americanization of the English Language Parochial School," New York History 53 (April 1972): 157-177; Michael Feldberg, The Philadelphia Bible Riots of 1844: A Study of Ethnic Conflict (Westport, Conn., 1975); and two studies by Mary J. Oates: "Organized Volunteerism: The Catholic Sisters in Massachusetts, 1870-1940," American Quarterly 30 (Winter 1978): 652-680, and Learning to Teach: The Professional Preparation of Massachusetts Parochial School Faculty, 1870-1940, Cushwa Center Working Papers (Notre Dame, 1981).

Jay Dolan also served as the editor of an important collection of reprints and original titles on "The American Catholic Tradition." The series includes a variety of books on diverse aspects of American Catholicism. The story of Catholic parochial education and parish life was prominent among them. Of particular value to the historiography of parochial education are three titles in the series: Robert Emmett Curran, S.J., Michael Augustine Corrigan and the Shaping of Conservative Catholicism in America, 1878-1902 (New York, 1978); Mary Ewens, The Role of the Nun in Nineteenth Century America (New York, 1978); and Bernard Julius Meiring, Educational Aspects of the Legislation of the Councils of Baltimore, 1829-1884 (New York, 1978). In addition, several other titles in the series touch on educational topics and the entire series is worthy of consideration by any scholar interested in the history of American Catholicism.

Secondary sources on parochial education in Chicago and Milwaukee are of relatively high quality when one considers the paucity of primary source materials. The topic has captured the interest of a number of first-rate historians and the future is promising. The books and articles on Catholicism and Catholic education in these two archdioceses range from helpful to excellent.

Studies of all aspects of Chicago history have appeared with great regularity in recent years. Dependable background information is available in Bessie Louise Pierce, A History of Chicago (3 vols., New York, 1937-1957). Every historian of that great city owes Pierce a debt of gratitude. Her books are consistently valuable on the development of the Church in the years from 1833 to 1893. Less dependable but full of interesting details is A. T. Andreas, A History of Chicago (3 vols., Chicago, 1886). Finally researchers will want to consult Harold M. Mayer and Richard C. Wade, Chicago: The Growth of a Metropolis (Chicago, 1969) and a forthcoming companion volume on the people of Chicago by Perry Duis. These volumes provide a rich pictorial perspective on the development of the nation's "second city."

The history of Chicago Catholicism has had several patrons, both early and late. Foremost has been the pioneering work of Gilbert J. Garraghan, S.J., professor of history at Loyola University of Chicago. Garraghan spent several decades researching and writing the history of his Church in his city.   He established and edited the Illinois Catholic Historical Review (now known as Mid-America) to encourage a deeper appreciation of the Catholic past among scholars and lay people.   The Garraghan legacy also lives on in several works including The Catholic Church in Chicago, 1637-1871 (Chicago, 1921) and The Jesuits in the Middle United States (3 vols., New York, 1938).

Others worked with Garraghan in his mission.   James J. Thompson published Antecedents of the Archdiocese of Chicago (Chicago, 1921) which brought together a wide variety of information on Chicago's parishes.   Thompson's work has recently been superseded by Harry C. Koenig's edition, A History of the Parishes of the Archdiocese of Chicago (Chicago, 1980).   Still useful is Daniel Kucera's Church-State Relationships in Education in Illinois (Washington, D. C., 1955).

In recent years a trio of University of Chicago graduates have published exceptional studies of different aspects of Catholicism in Chicago.   James W. Sanders' Education of an Urban Minority: Catholics in Chicago, 1833-1965 (New York, 1977) is a first-rate survey of parochial education, especially in the twentieth century.   Charles Shanabruch published Chicago's Catholics: The Evolution of an American Identity (Notre Dame, 1981), an exploration of the turbulent social history of the Church in that city in the years from 1843 to 1920.   Edward R. Kantowicz picks up that story in his Corporation Sole: Cardinal Mundelein and Chicago Catholicism (Notre Dame, 1982).   This prize-winning book is more than a biography.   In fact the book is a penetrating analysis   of   the   changing   nature   of   diocesan   leadership   and diocesan   decision-making   in   Chicago   and   other   archdioceses. Kantowicz   shows   how   Mundelein   and   his   brother   builder   bishops shaped twentieth century Catholicism in the United States.

Milwaukee has not had the same amount of attention from historians as Chicago.   Yet several general works are worthy of attention.   Bayard   Still's   Milwaukee: The   History   of   a   City (Madison, 1948) is a bit dated, but still the most useful and dependable history of the city available.   Also of note is Gerd Korman's Immigrants, Industrialists, and Americanizers: The View from Milwaukee, 1866-1920 (Madison, 1965) and Lloyd P. Jorgenson, The Founding of Public Education in Wisconsin (Madison, 1956). The most penetrating analysis of Wisconsin's major city is to be found   in   the   work   of   Kathleen   Neils   Conzen,   particularly Immigrant Milwaukee, 1836-1860: Accommodation and Community in a Frontier City (Cambridge, 1976).

Milwaukee has also been a topic of some interest to Catholic historical researchers.   In fact, the aforementioned Peter Leo Johnson made something of a cottage industry out of Milwaukee Catholic history.   During his long and fruitful career, Johnson published many books and articles on his archdiocese.   Of particular note are the following: Stuffed Saddlebags: The Life of Martin Kundig, Priest, 1805-1879 (Milwaukee, 1942); Centennial Essays   for   the   Milwaukee   Archdiocese,   1843-1943   (Milwaukee, 1943);   The   Daughters   of   Charity   in   Milwaukee,   1846-1946 (Milwaukee,   1946);   Halcyon   Days: The   Story   of   St.   Francis Seminary,   1856-1956   (Milwaukee,   1956);   and   Crosier   on   the

Frontier: A Life of John Martin Henni (Madison, 1959).   In
addition to these titles, Johnson published dozens of essays in
the pages of Salesianum, the Wisconsin Magazine of History, and
other scholarly journals.

Johnson was not alone in his efforts. In fact, he had been
preceded by Harry Heming, who edited The Catholic Church in
Wisconsin (4 vols., Milwaukee, 1895-1899). Also useful on the
history of the Church in Milwaukee is M. Justille McDonald's The
Irish in Wisconsin During the Nineteenth Century (Washington,
D. C.. 1948) and Benjamin Blied's Three Archbishops of Milwaukee
(Milwaukee, 1955). An excellent biography is M. Mileta Ludwig's
Right Hand Glove Uplifted: The Life of the Right Reverend Michael
Heiss (New York, 1968). It goes without saying that a great deal
remains to be done on the history of Catholicism in Milwaukee.

IV

It would not be an overstatement to refer to the 1970s as
the "renaissance" of American Catholic historical research. More
was accomplished in the last decade than in the previous century.
Certainly the keynote of this progress was the 1974 statement on
ecclesiastical archives from the National Conference of Catholic
Bishops. Made aware of the Catholic contribution to American
culture by the forthcoming bicentennial anniversary of American
independence, the bishops called for "a nationwide effort to preserve and organize all existing records and papers that can be
found in chancery offices, general and provincial houses of religious orders and institutions of our country." As part of this

effort, the NCCB recommended that each residential bishop appoint a properly qualified individual to serve as diocesan archivist and expressed the hope that the bishops would grant access to diocesan archival materials to qualified researchers. The bishops reminded all Catholics "of their obligation to hand down to posterity the record of those accomplishments for the Church and the nation."

This brief, forthright document was the stimulus for the establishment of many new diocesan archival programs. The number of priests, religious, and laity attending archival education programs increased dramatically in the 1970s. In fact, the number of diocesan archival programs more than doubled in the four years after the dissemination of the NCCB statement and the number of diocesan and religious archivists has grown large enough to justify the compilation and publication of the Catholic Archives Newsletter. Presently the number of diocesan archival programs is fast approaching one hundred.

Catholic diocesan archival programs were not the only repositories to be refurbished during the 1970s. Religious congregations of women also joined in the effort to preserve and make available the archival materials that document their substantial service to the Church. Under the auspices of the Leadership Conference of Women Religious, Evangeline Thomas, C.S.J., directed a program that trained 375 archivists representing hundreds of congregations across the country, surveyed the archival holdings of those and other congregations, and published the invaluable Women Religious History Sources: A Guide to Repositories in the United

States. No other volume brings together as much information on the history of women's religious congregations in the United States.

Other organizations and individuals have also contributed to this renaissance. The establishment of the Cushwa Center for the Study of American Catholicism at the University of Notre Dame has given momentum to Catholic historical research through the publication of a newsletter, a working papers series, and an annual book competition, as well as through a substantial research grant program. The U. S. Catholic Historian, the lively quarterly sponsored by the U. S. Catholic Historical Society, has provided yet another outlet for the fruits of Catholic historical scholarship. Researchers interested in learning more about what has been published in the field can consult two recent and helpful bibliographies: James Hennesey, comp., American Catholic Bibliography, 1970-1982 (2 parts, Notre Dame, 1982-1983), and John Tracy Ellis and Robert Trisco, eds., A Guide to American Catholic History (2nd ed., Santa Barbara, Calif., 1982).

"We stand on the verge of a major expansion of our understanding of the history of Catholics in this country," notes James O'Toole, " and the continued cooperation among archivists and historians will make that expansion possible." Indeed, that prophecy is already a fact and James Hennesey's American Catholics: A History of the Roman Catholic Community in the United States (New York, 1981) is solid evidence. Yet Catholic scholars must guard against a feeling of smug satisfaction. "American Catholic historiography," notes James Hennesey, "if it remains

fairly set in its ways and preoccupations, likewise remains
heavily parochial in regard to the publishers and the journals it
employs." Hennesey is quite correct; witness the fact that not a
single study of American Catholicism is cited in the American
Historical Association's recent assessment of historical
scholarship, <u>The Past Before Us: Contemporary Historical Writing
in the United States</u> (Ithaca, NY, 1980). The mission of Catholic
historians in the future, therefore, must be to integrate Catholic historical research into the mainstream of American historiography.

Biographical Note

Timothy Walch is Associate Editor of the U. S. Catholic Historian, the award-winning journal of the U. S. Catholic Historical Society. He is also Editor of Prologue: Journal of the National Archives and an administrator with the National Archives and Records Administration in Washington, D. C.

Educated at the University of Notre Dame and Northwestern University, Dr. Walch is the author or editor of six books and more than two dozen articles on archival and historical topics. His most recent book is Catholicism in America: A Social History, forthcoming from Robert E. Kreiger Publishing Co.

The Heritage of
American Catholicisim